Cartomancy and Celtic Symbolism

An Essential Guide to Card Divination and Ancient Pagan Symbols

© Copyright 2024 - All rights reserved.

The contents of this book may not be reproduced, duplicated, or transmitted without direct written permission from the author.

Under no circumstances will any legal responsibility or blame be held against the publisher for any reparation, damages, or monetary loss due to the information herein, either directly or indirectly.

Legal Notice:

You cannot amend, distribute, sell, use, quote, or paraphrase any part or the content within this book without the consent of the author.

Disclaimer Notice:

Please note the information contained within this document is for educational and entertainment purposes only. No warranties of any kind are expressed or implied. Readers acknowledge that the author is not engaging in the rendering of legal, financial, medical, or professional advice. Please consult a licensed professional before attempting any techniques outlined in this book.

By reading this document, the reader agrees that under no circumstances is the author responsible for any losses, direct or indirect, which are incurred as a result of the use of the information contained within this document, including, but not limited to, errors, omissions, or inaccuracies.

Your Free Gift
(only available for a limited time)

Thanks for getting this book! If you want to learn more about various spirituality topics, then join Mari Silva's community and get a free guided meditation MP3 for awakening your third eye. This guided meditation mp3 is designed to open and strengthen ones third eye so you can experience a higher state of consciousness. Simply visit the link below the image to get started.

https://spiritualityspot.com/meditation

Or, Scan the QR code!

Table of Contents

PART 1: CARTOMANCY 1
   INTRODUCTION 2
   CHAPTER 1: THE ART OF CARTOMANCY 3
   CHAPTER 2: CHOOSING A DECK 12
   CHAPTER 3: SYMBOLISM AND MEANINGS 21
   CHAPTER 4: SPREADS AND LAYOUTS 33
   CHAPTER 5: COMBINATIONS AND REVERSED CARDS 42
   CHAPTER 6: PERFORMING A READING 52
   CHAPTER 7: SAMPLE READINGS 61
   CHAPTER 8: INTUITIVE READINGS 68
   CHAPTER 9: ADVANCED CARTOMANCY 76
   CHAPTER 10: DIFFERENT APPROACHES TO CARTOMANCY 82
   CONCLUSION 89
PART 2: CELTIC SYMBOLISM 90
   INTRODUCTION 91
   CHAPTER 1: THE ANCIENT CELTS 93
   CHAPTER 2: CELTIC BELIEFS AND SYMBOLISM 103
   CHAPTER 3: A-Z OF CELTIC SYMBOLS 112
   CHAPTER 4: THE CELTIC TREE CALENDAR 131
   CHAPTER 5: THE OGHAM ALPHABET 148
   CHAPTER 6: THE WHEEL OF THE YEAR 165
   CHAPTER 7: THE TREE OF LIFE 177
   CHAPTER 8: ANIMALS AS CELTIC SYMBOLS 186

CHAPTER 9: CELTIC DIVINATION 194
BONUS: TREE MEDITATIONS 204
CONCLUSION 212
HERE'S ANOTHER BOOK BY MARI SILVA THAT YOU MIGHT LIKE 215
YOUR FREE GIFT (ONLY AVAILABLE FOR A LIMITED TIME) 216
REFERENCES 217
IMAGE SOURCES 226

Part 1: Cartomancy

Unlocking the Secrets of Divination Using Playing Cards

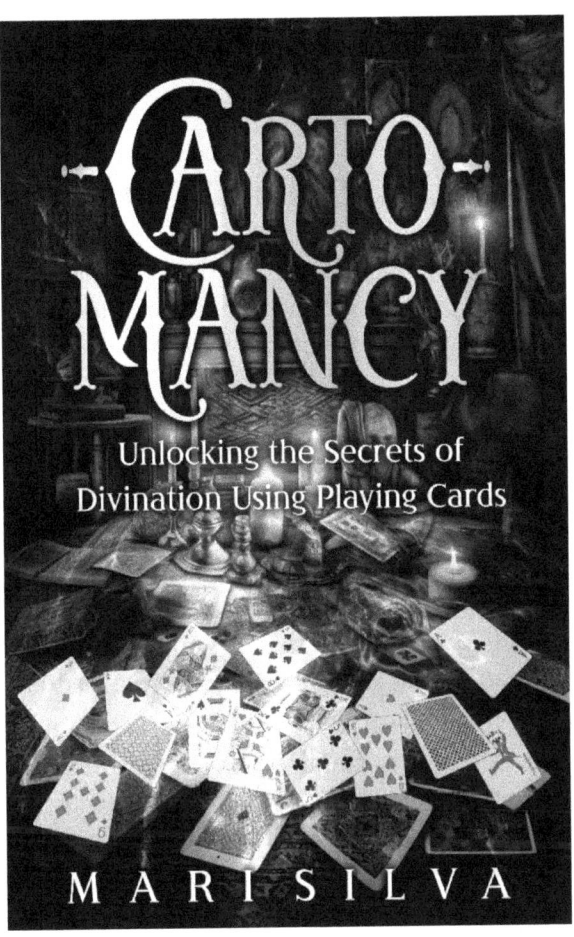

Introduction

For a very long time, many have looked to the cards to divine life's secrets. There's a good reason people have turned to cards to get the answers they seek and to receive guidance in life, and that is because, when you know how to work with these cards, the answers you receive can have a profound impact on your life.

In this book, you'll discover everything you need to know about cartomancy and how to become a professional. Unlike other books in the market, this book is written in easy-to-understand English. It offers you hands-on instructions on how to perfect this craft. You're not going to be left confused about what to do at any point in time. This is because the book has been written to ensure that, whether you are a beginner or proficient at cartomancy, you will know exactly what to do at every turn.

You'll learn everything about this craft, from its rich and storied history to the meanings of the cards you'll be working with to clarify your life. While this book doesn't promise to teach you how to predict the future to a "T," it will help you learn how you can sense the energies of the cards and use them to ensure you always make the right choices in your life that will lead to the positive outcomes you seek, whether that's in your finances, love life, health, or any other matter.

If you are absolutely ready to begin understanding the life that you have lived, and if you are prepared to take your life to the next level by choosing the right course of action to gain the things you want, then head on to chapter one.

Chapter 1: The Art of Cartomancy

Tarot cards were used as a form of divination.[1]

Once Upon a Time in Europe...

The first time playing cards existed was in Europe in the 1360s, particularly in Eastern Germany and Central Italy. By 1371, these cards were in Spain, where they were known as *naïpes*, which the Spanish still call these cards to this day. Back then, Fernando de la Torre designed a special form of the cards. According to him, these cards made it possible to predict your fortunes. He told people they could figure out who yearned for them the most, who was the most admired and wanted, and many other things. The Spanish would refer to telling fortunes as *echar suertes*, which translates to "casting lots." This is the earliest record of this term being used relating to card playing.

It's not clear how people used cards to predict their fortunes. At least there were no clear explanations until over 150 years later. However, before then, the cards would be classed with dice and other divination methods as *sortilege*, a word for witchcraft, often explicitly used to describe divination. Giovanni Francesco Pico Della Mirandola, an Italian, wrote passionately against the craft of divination in 1506. In his writings, he included pictures that were part of card games, naming them abominable. 48 years later, Martin de Azpilcueta, a Spanish priest, would officially declare all cards (also known as cartas) as evil and the process of divination using these cards as sinful and subject to condemnation. Also, Juan Perez de Montalvàn believed that fortune-telling using cards was witchcraft.

Unfortunately, there was no clear description by any of these men about how the cards were used to predict fortunes. For this reason, it's unclear whether they were talking about cartomancy or condemning something else altogether. In the 16th century, certain books were dedicated to fortune telling, which you could use to understand the cards and other things like dice and spinners. These books had pictures on the cards, which didn't play a significant part in divination and couldn't be classified under cartomancy.

One popular, simple card fortune book printed in 1505 is the Mainzer Kartenlosbuch. This book connects every card of the 48 cards in the German deck with a fortune written in eight lines. Interestingly, these fortunes were simply adaptations from some other, earlier fortune book that was not based on cards. The way people would consult this book was to first draw a card and then look at the book to figure out their fortune. Alternatively, they would attach a spinner to the book, which was split into

48 different parts, each with the card's name. Many of these European books from the late 15th to the 16th century were produced and written in various languages.

Simultaneously, the first record of divination by tarot would be during that century. Teofilo Folengo, also known as Merlin Coccai, kept a record of this divination in his interesting allegory, Chaos del Triperuno, which he wrote in 1527. The participants in the reading had explained the meaning of the cards they had received to a character named Limerno. They wanted him to write sonnets for them based on the cards they had drawn. Limerno would go on to oblige them. This was a work of fiction, but then, it's clear that Teofilo had some ideas about how cards could be used to figure out what life may hold in store, and this is the ultimate goal of cartomancy. This is as good a time as any to specify that cartomancy should not be treated as a way to tell your fortune or predict to the letter how things will work out for you on a particular day or regarding a specific situation. Instead, think of the readings as more of a guide and not the ultimate law on what will befall you.

Another record on cartomancy is from 1538, thanks to Juan Luis Vives, who explained in writing that one could consider the picture on a card as a sign of their future. He wrote a scene showing two people playing cards which alluded to this idea. Granted, the concept of divination was casually touched upon in this scene, but that implies that this must have been a common thing that occurred back then. In those times, looking at the cards to learn things to come was not novel.

The First Recorded Readings

Actual card readings would begin to show up in the early 1600s. From these times, the earliest records of how to divine the future with cards exist, and among the earliest explanations of the process was written by Sir John Melton. He wrote Astrologaster, or, The Figure Caster, in 1620. He went on to talk about how Henry Cuffee met his end for being treasonous in 1601 and that some wizard had already predicted his death 20 years beforehand by using cards. The wizard had asked the unfortunate Henry to choose three cards from a deck with all Knaves. Then he placed the cards one after the other on the table, face down. After this, he was asked to pick one, then another, and look at the face of each card. The record states that when Henry looked at the cards, he wasn't seeing Knaves. His own face stared back at him from the first card, the second card showed his judge, and the final one had the scene where he would be executed in Tyburn.

In 1942, Sebastián Cirac Estopañán documented the Spanish Inquisition, and his work contains information on how 16th-century women practiced card reading. Still, these weren't in-depth descriptions, sadly. When Margarita de Borja was tried for witchcraft in Madrid from 1615 to 1617, she confessed that she helped her clients by reading cards for them. The way she described it, she'd recite an incantation to Saint Martha as she shuffled the cards first, then set the cards on the table in five rows of four cards each, all face-up. It was a good sign if the cards appeared in pairs (for instance, a Knave with a Knave or a Queen with a Queen). If they didn't, it was a bad omen.

Yet another person who was tried for witchcraft from 1631 to 1632 in Toledo was Mariá Castellanos. Her process also involved an incantation as she shuffled the cards and set twelve cards on the table. She aimed to see if the Jack and Knight of Clubs wound up beside each other. Tried in 1633, Lady Antonia Mejía de Acosta said she would remove the Nine of Clubs out of a 40-card deck and then shuffle the other 39 as she prayed. When she had finished, she would set out nine cards. If there were more Cups and Coins than Clubs and Swords, that was a good omen, but it was unfortunate if the cards didn't turn up that way.

There would be yet another witch trial that lasted from 1648 to 1649. The unfortunate victim of this trial was Lady María de Acevedo. Working with 41 cards, she could figure out what her significant other was up to whenever he went to the palace. She could tell what thoughts occupied his mind, and not only that, but she could also use the cards to influence him so that he would return to her after any argument they had. In fact, she shared a story of a woman who was married to a water bearer struggling to make ends meet. The woman needed to know if her husband had fallen for someone else. During the reading, the King of Cups and the Jack of Coins showing up together would be a good omen, as the former represented the husband while the latter was the wife. These cards together meant all was well on the love front. The woman shuffled the deck of cards and set them down one after the other in five rows, all face up. Sadly, she learned the worst from this reading. She would shuffle the cards three more times, yet the Knight of Cups and Jack of Coins never showed up as a pair. Go through the Spanish Inquisition, and you'll find many readings of this sort recorded up until the 19th century.

With time, the witches would work with the cards by shuffling them while praying or saying incantations, placing 13 cards on the table in a circle and one in the middle. The reading would be founded on the magical qualities of the first five cards drawn. Still, there's no further information about what would happen. In 1960, Dorman Newman of England created a deck of cards meant to be used for divination. His design had the fortunes written on the cards themselves. It would eventually be published once more, in 1711, by John Lenthall. These cards would wind up having several iterations.

Sometimes, what appeared to be a simple card game was actually divination. The popular game Solitaire, for instance, is thought of as initially having been a form of cartomancy. Solitaire is called *Reéssite* in France (a word that means "success"), and many people want to find out if they will attain success using the cards.

Solitaire wasn't the only version of divination, as there could be more than one "player" in a card reading. For instance, in Whartoniana, Miscellanies, in verse and prose, published in 1727, a chapter talks about a curious game known as Piquet. It was no ordinary game, as it involved divination on heart matters. The author wrote of his experience with a character named Theresius. He chose to visit this character because he was curious about his destiny. So, Theresius read his palm, cast lots based on astrology, and then asked the author to return the next day. The author obliged but was confused when Theresius asked him to play Piquet. He went along with it, and eventually, Theresius played the Queen of Hearts, which won him the game. When this happened, Theresius revealed to the author that if he intended to fall in love, it was important that he went after a woman who was more suited to him because, as he put it, "For if ever you attack the divine Pallas, you will infallibly lurch."

By 1730, cartomancy would be practiced with regular cards. The first depiction of this was in the English play Jack the Gyant-Killer. The author talked about using a deck of 52 cards. First, the reader would need to choose the Significator card after shuffling the deck, and then four Kings were assigned to this card. Then the deck needed to be cut. After this, the pack was laid out in at least three rows, and the Significator card had to be found. Once the card was spotted, the reader interpreted the surrounding cards. According to this play, the Spades were the only suit that meant bad luck.

About 20 years later, a document would describe another method of reading Tarot cards in Bologna. This method involved 35 cards split into groups of seven. The manuscript explains what each of the cards meant. Still, there's no straightforward narrative surrounding the groupings, so it's unclear if this was a commonly used method for cartomancy in Bologna in the 18th century. Eventually, the card readers in this region would opt to work with 45 cards out of 62 cards, but they'd never use the same cards across all spreads.

Later in the 1750s, cartomancy would be recorded again, this time by Oliver Goldsmith in his book The Vicar of Wakefield. He wrote that cartomancy was something to be considered admirable when a woman had the skill, one he deemed as valuable as reading, writing, music, and needlework, among other things. At this time, there was also a description of cartomancy in Russia written by Giacomo Casanova. He had a mistress named Zaïre – and she was only thirteen. He thought she was acting suspiciously and criticized her for constantly referencing the cards, which he claimed she would consult ten times daily. He claimed he would have stayed with her if it weren't for her "desperate jealousy" and "blind trust" of the cards. Apparently, this young girl had figured out how to tell what he'd been up to whenever he was out all night. He would eventually throw her cards into the fire.

The first record of cartomancy in France came in the 18th century in the form of a police record dated March 17, 1759. Two women were imprisoned for eight days because, according to the reports, they had scammed other people of their money by pretending to help them find whatever they'd lost using divination by cards. Then, in 1972 in Marseille, Anne Cauvin would also be sentenced. She endured being "exposed in shackles" for three days, with her head in a bonnet covered in tarot cards. They also put a sieve on her neck, and she had to remain this way for an hour each time before the executioner would step in to break the sieve and rip up the cards. Thus, at this time, it's evident that cartomancy was popular, but it was usually done in secret.

Out of the Darkness, into the Light

Jean-Baptiste Alliette, born 1738, died 1791, was known as Etteilla, his last name reversed. In a book Etteilla wrote the year he died, he talked about cartomancy, which he called "*cartonomancy*." He claimed no one knew of the practice in France until three old people offered their services in 1751,

1752, and 1753. According to Etteilla, the clients of these strangers had to draw their cards one after the other, and all omens were interpreted according to suits. Drawing Hearts meant happiness, Diamonds meant country, Clubs meant money, and Spades implied sorrow.

Etteilla claimed that he was the one who elevated the practice of cartomancy by doing away with picking cards one after the other and, instead, conducting readings based on the entire deck laid out on the table. Obviously, from what you now know of the history of cartomancy, you can tell Etteilla was appropriating credit that wasn't his. However, you can agree that he was the first to put out a printed cartomancy methodology in 1770, which wasn't attached to a pack like the Newman-Lenthall deck of cards. His publication would prove very popular, and he was the one who gave each pip an interpretation rather than just working with a card or two based on the suit's meaning.

In Eteilla's first publication, he shared a method of working with 32 cards using a French Piquet deck with every pip except the ones from 2 to 6. He would also add another card as the generic Significator, which he eponymously named "the Etteilla." He gave each card its meaning and keyword. He shared valuable information about various layouts like squares (Zaïre's favorite) or fans. He also briefly touched on working with Tarot cards for divination. Still, he never gave an in-depth description of the process.

In 1772, Antoine Court de Gébelin worked with another author who remained anonymous to put out some essays on the Tarot and its esoteric significance. The anonymous author was responsible for crafting a method of cartomancy that would work with Tarot, prompting Etteilla to pivot to the Tarot itself and tout its benefits. He would make it more complicated by adding some astrology in conjunction with his custom design of the Tarot. After this, he would publish works criticizing others' approaches to the Tarot, and with his notoriety, he drew a bunch of devotees committed to learning from him between 1783 and 1791. Thanks to Eteilla's obvious narcissism and De Gébelin's essays, Europe would eventually become aware of Tarot and other related esoteric matters and cartomancy. Etteilla's devotees made it their mission to spread his ideas far and wide and, with them, his custom Tarot deck.

Marie-Ann Adélaïde Lenormand became the most famous cartomancer during France's Revolution. Born in 1772, she was known as Mademoiselle Lenormand, and she kept that title Mademoiselle until she died in 1843, as she never got married. Lenormand developed her reputation, much like Etteilla did, through self-promotion. When she was a teenager, she realized she was clairvoyant. Lenormand used that gift to make herself a fortune during the Revolution. She became even more famous when Empress Josephine reached out to her for her services, and from there, other members of high society reached out to her. Her clientele included those in the most influential and powerful social circles of the time. She would write that she had done work for some of the crème de la crème. However, today, it is known that she was a card reader for Josephine and Napoleon and the author of the popular Le Petit Lenormand and Le Grand Lenormand oracle cards. Even now, these cards are used in France and French-speaking places. Still, the odds are she didn't really have anything to do with the cards, and the manufacturers are simply making money from her name since she's long gone.

Cartomancy in Modern Times

In the 19th century, cartomancy with Tarot would become more popular, far more so than working with regular playing cards, Etteilla's cards, and Lenormand cards. The English considered Tarot as an occult matter. Arthur Edward Waite, an English mystic, had difficulty finding real Tarot cards, so he devised his pack for telling fortunes, working with Pamela Colman Smith, who handled the artwork. Smith came up with some beautiful designs, and thanks to this and the fact that all the pips had illustrations, Tarot would become the popular choice for cartomancy, especially in the anglophone world.

Over in France, the people use either 22 cards out of the Tarot de Marseille or standard playing cards. Come 1900, there was a more modern pack of Tarot, which had double-ended genre illustrations. Also, the pips were your usual Hearts, Spades, Diamonds, and Clubs. Oswald Wirth, an occultist, redesigned and printed the Tarot de Marseille Trumps in 1889. In 1927, he published a revised form that included text and which many cartomancers would adopt. Paul Marteau would direct Grimaud, a card-making firm, to revive the Tarot de Marseille in 1930. After this, Marteau published a guide to the new pack in 1949 entitled Le Tarot de Marseille. Cartomancy is practiced in many different styles, and it's still evolving. Every form of cartomancy springs from the English or French occult interests of the late 19th century — except for Bolognese Tarotmancy, of course.

Differences between Tarot Reading and Cartomancy

Tarot reading and cartomancy are about reading cards to figure out what the future could bring, but there's so much more involved. Tarot is well recognized, and the decks tend to be large with interesting cards rather than the sort you'd find in the common card decks. Plus, tarot card decks have Wands, Pentacles, Cups, and Swords *as suits*. You'll also find Knights and common Jacks, which aren't in your run-of-the-mill deck.

Cartomancy is card reading with regular cards. The Queens represent female energies, while the Kings represent masculine energies. The Jacks are youths and don't have a specific gender. Cartomancy can offer some accuracy when predicting when something will likely play out. Where the Tarot deck has 78 cards, cartomancy readings usually work with a standard deck of 52 cards. Also, you can expect the meanings you get from cartomancy to be more to the point than Tarot. If you want to understand the possible results of your situation, use Tarot. But to get specific answers, cartomancy is best.

One More Thing...

This is an excellent time to remind you that whether it's cartomancy or Tarot reading, you must understand that this practice isn't about accuracy in seeing the future or making predictions, so please do not base important life decisions on the cards alone. Instead, work with them as powerful guidance, growth, and self-discovery tools. When you do a reading or sit in one, you must understand all you're getting is a possible outcome or path heavily influenced by your present emotions and choices. This means the readings aren't set in stone — and that's likely a relief since it means you can always do something about negative readings.

Now that you know the rich origins of cards as divinatory tools, how do you choose the right deck before you start? How many decks are there? Which one's relevant? You're going to learn all this and more in the following chapter.

Chapter 2: Choosing a Deck

Traditional Decks Versus Modified and Specialized Decks

If you've ever played Poker or some other card game, you may not have realized then that you were playing with the original version of the tarot. This deck has 52 cards of four suits: Spades, Hearts, Diamonds, and Clubs. Each suit has numbered cards from 2 through 9, the Ace card, and the face cards, the King, Queen, and Jack. It is said that these suits are connected to the classical elements:

- Earth (Clubs)
- Air (Diamonds)
- Fire (Hearts)
- Water (Spades)

There are various designs of traditional playing card decks these days. One of the common traditional decks is the French-suited one. Clubs or clovers are known as *Trèfles,* Diamonds (or Tiles) are called *Carreaux,* Hearts are known as *Cœurs,* and Spades (or Pikes) are called *Piques.* The Queen or Lady card is the Dame, the King is the Roi, and the Jack or Knave is the Valet. There's also another card known as the Cavalier between the Queen and the Jack. The French-suited cards are common because their simple patterns make it easier to mass-produce them. It's also worth noting that the French connect their face cards to specific personalities. If you're interested, look at the correlations below:

Suits: Clubs, Diamonds, Hearts, Spades
Kings: Alexandre, César, Charles, David
Queens: Argine, Rachel, Judith, Pallas
Jacks: Lancelot, Hector, La Hire, Hogier

Then there are the Belgian-Genoese cards, the second most common traditional deck of cards worldwide. These cards don't have the names the French assign to the face cards. These cards became common in the Ottoman Empire when the rulership permitted card playing. Eventually, the cards would be found in the Middle East, North Africa, and the Balkans.

Modified decks are almost like traditional decks, but they're changed in some way to make them easier to use for cartomancy. For instance, some decks may have extra cards, or the artwork may be modified to flesh out the readings for more details. The specialized cards, however, are specifically for cartomancy, with beautiful, exquisite art that offers more meaning thanks to the symbolism of each element of the drawing on the card. You can also expect these decks to have extra cards and different suits.

Standard Bicycle Deck

The Ace of Spades in a Bicycle card deck has special branding.[2]

The Bicycle Playing Cards are made by the United States Printing Company, with the first decks ever printed in 1885. The deck is called "Bicycle" because of the back design on the first issue, which displayed penny-farthings. If you're wondering what "penny-farthings" are, they're an early type of bicycle with high wheels at the front and small wheels at the back. They were also known as ordinary high-wheelers or high wheels.

But, back to the matter of the Bicycle deck. It has 52 cards, reds, and blacks, belonging to any of the four classical suits. The numbers go from 2 to 10 and end with the Jack card. The Ace of Spades has the Bicycle branding on it. Usually, this deck has poker hand ranks, 2 Jokers, and an informational card. For the most part, custom Bicycle cards have 2 extra cards along with the Jokers, which magicians use for tricks or advertising.

Gypsy Witch Deck

The Gypsy Witch Deck.[8]

The Gypsy Witch Fortune Telling Playing Cards were first published in 1904, and they're still being used today. They're older than the common Rider-Waite deck, which would first be published 5 years later. This deck is fascinating because it is inspired by Madam Lenormand herself. If you do your homework, you'll find many decks crafted in line with Lenormand's ideas, using mnemonic pictures on the cards. For some reason, these pictures and their interpretations don't align with the generally accepted interpretations of the suits or their numbers. These cards are also known as oracle cards and are a copy of the decks that came out after Lenormand died.

This deck comprises the same cards you'd find in a standard deck, except each card has a picture and interpretation. The images are reminiscent of the Victorian era, with the illustration style of the time making the cards even more interesting than other decks. Since the cards are already interpreted, and the meanings are right on them for you to read, you may assume that it would be easy to work with them since you don't have to memorize the interpretations, but that's not the case. Usually, in cartomancy, the suits have specific meanings.

For instance, the Hearts are about matters of the heart and other emotions. The Diamonds are about money and finances, and so on. However, with the Gypsy Witch Deck, you can't find any correlation between the pips and numbers and the images or interpretations. For instance, the 10 of Diamonds has a picture of a scythe and a bale of hay, and the interpretation reads, "The Scythe presages disappointment and when near the coffin, early death." Finding the correlation between that interpretation and the idea of Diamonds is pretty confusing.

Lenormand Deck

Lenormand cards are more practical in cartomancy.'

The Lenormand deck is like Tarot in that it's used in cartomancy, but that's about it in terms of similarities. The Lenormand is much more practical because it's not about the impressions you get from looking at each one and is more about what goes on in your daily life. In other words, this deck is excellent when you want insight into practical affairs. Where Tarot is about the *why*, Lenormand is about the *how*; this deck has 36 cards, and it's the best option if you'd rather have clarity from your readings, especially when you draw the cards in pairs rather than singles. When you work with these alongside Tarot interpretations, you'd be hard-pressed to find any better way to find clarity in cartomancy.

Fin de Siècle Kipper

The new iteration of Kipper cards depicts important life events.[5]

Kipper cards are common in Germany and, similar to the Lenormand, have been in use since the mid-19th century. A new iteration of this Kipper deck is that by Ciro Marchetti, which is elegant in its presentation. This deck has 36 cards depicting essential life events and situations that most people find relatable, like being ill, taking a trip, working, getting married, etc. This deck is direct and easy to interpret, so even if you're new to cartomancy, you should have no problem figuring out what the cards mean. For instance, you have the High Honors card, which shows the King bestowing honor on a man kneeling before him. Or there's the marriage card, with a man and a woman dressed in wedding outfits.

To read Kipper cards, you can draw single cards. Usually, they're read in a straight line, and an odd number of cards is drawn (typically five or seven). It's also important to note the placement of the cards and how close they are to each other on the line, as these factors affect the reading. You also have to pay attention to the direction. Say, for instance, you draw the Gift card, and it's before the Main Male card. That could mean the man will get a gift. However, if the Gift card comes after the Main Male card, it could mean the man himself is offering someone else the gift. You read oracle and Tarot decks using intuition and interpret Lenormand cards metaphorically. However, Kipper cards are to be interpreted literally.

These are just a few of the decks you can use for divination. However, you should never forget that you can choose any other design or deck you want. It all comes down to your goals, preferences, and personal interests. Whether you prefer smaller or larger cards, more or fewer cards in your decks, or more or less flexibility in interpreting your cards, you should go with whatever resonates with you.

Choosing Your Deck

When choosing your deck, you must settle on something you're happy with. This means working with your intuition rather than choosing the first or only available deck you see. Here are some helpful tips to guide you.

First, you need to think about what you prefer. Everyone is different regarding the sort of symbolism and imagery they resonate with. Consider whether you'd rather have something more traditional or classic, like the Rider-Waite deck, for instance, or something more modern. Besides just the designs, consider what you want to accomplish with the deck. Do you want the kind that gives you straightforward interpretations? Or would you prefer something that is layered in meaning? These are questions you need to ask yourself as you make your choice.

Next, you need to do your homework. As you now know, different decks have different features. You need to think about what works best for you, but not only that, you should seek out others' opinions as well. For instance, check out fora and threads on cartomancy on Reddit, or look at the various reviews for each sort of deck. Also, look up the images of the deck's cards first to know if you'd be happy working with them. If you're still confused about which to choose, looking into the history of the decks may also help you figure out what works for you.

Now, you've got to interview the cards. Scratching your head at this one? That's understandable, but it shouldn't be strange. If the cards can tell you something about what to expect in life, there's no reason they can't tell you whether or not you'll work well with them! Therefore, you need to interview the deck before you settle on it. This means you need to ask it questions and then draw some cards to answer them. During this interview, your job is to observe how the deck offers you answers because, believe it or not, each deck has a unique personality. Just as certain personalities blend well together while others clash, one or the other scenario may occur with you and your cards.

How do you interview cards? Make them fill out a questionnaire or something? What you need to do is shuffle the cards. At the same time, you set your intention firmly in your mind; to become familiar with the deck's personality. When you've finished shuffling, it's time for your questions. Here are some of the things you could ask:

- What's your usual energy?
- What are the good things about you?
- What do you intend to do during readings?
- What do you have to teach me, if anything?
- What's the best way to work with each other?

With each question you ask, you should draw a card. Don't be in a hurry to interpret what each card means. Take your time and allow the answer to bubble up within you from your intuition. This way, you'll have an accurate grasp of the cards' energy and learn whether that's the deck you want to work with. This is just one way you can select or connect with a deck. There are other ways. For instance, you could:

1. **Spend some time with the deck.** The more you study each card and its symbolism, the more familiar it should become, and the better you can tell if it works for you. Shuffle the cards, handle them, and touch each one; their energy should connect with yours.

2. **Meditate with the deck of cards in your hands.** By meditating, you establish a connection with the cards on a profound level. If you like, you can bring the cards up to your heart energy center or chakra to feel their energy even better as you meditate. Also, the heart's intelligence will tell you immediately whether these cards are for you.

3. **Put the deck beneath your pillow** as you go to bed at night to get a sense of their energy. You can do this for several nights and pay particular attention to your dreams and how you feel when you wake up. When you sleep, your conscious mind goes offline. Your subconscious can pick up on subtle energies you miss at this time, carrying that information to you in your dreams or causing it to bubble up to your conscious mind when you awaken in the morning. Sleep is an excellent way to choose your deck.
4. **Draw your cards every day.** By doing this, you connect with the deck's energy, and you can observe how well the answers from the cards match your daily experiences.

Handling Your Deck

You need to be mindful of how you handle your deck, not just because you must keep them carefully but also because you must keep the energies pure during the reading. So, first of all, you must clear the deck of the energies from previous readings and any residual energies from anyone else who may have held the cards. Here are some ways you can clear the deck:

1. Shuffle the cards. The more thoroughly you shuffle them, the better the energy-clearing process.
2. Knock on the cards with your knuckles. Doing this will shake loose any old, stale energy lingering on the deck.
3. Smudge the deck. This means burning herbs like sage or palo santo and passing the cards through the smoke to eliminate negative and stale energies.
4. Finally, you can use visualization. Imagine a powerful golden light emanating from the palms of your hands and surrounding the deck, burning away any energy that doesn't belong there.

Maintaining and Protecting Your Cards

Keep the following in mind, and you'll have great-looking cards for a long time:

1. You need to treat your cards carefully so you don't damage them. Usually, the paper they're printed on is delicate, so you can't afford to be careless with them. Never crease the cards or bend them because that will not only not look good but will make it hard to

shuffle them.

2. Do your best to wash and dry your hands before you handle the cards. If oil, dirt, or other things get on your cards, it's not a good look. Inevitably, your cards will get stained despite your best intentions. In this case, remove the stain using a soft, gentle wipe.

3. Put the cards away where they belong when you've finished. Keep them in a pouch or a box when you aren't working with them. Also, don't let them suffer from the effects of humidity or extreme temperatures.

4. Finally, respect your cards. They're tools that allow you to communicate with divinity, so you should treat them with reverence. This has the added benefit of giving you more effective results when you work with them. Always be mindful and intentional in your dealings with the cards, and you'll find that they work with you, not against you, all the time.

Now you've learned about various decks and how to care for them, what are the deeper meanings of the cards? How can you know for sure what they're saying to you? Find out about this and more in the following chapter.

Chapter 3: Symbolism and Meanings

Regardless of the deck you work with or the card you're looking at, there's much symbolism surrounding cartomancy. This symbolism has lasted for centuries. In this chapter, you will discover the traditional meanings of each card, suit, and number. You'll discover what the court cards are about and the esoteric meanings inherent in every deck. As you read, remember that each card's interpretation and meaning can change depending on the context and reader.

The Four Suits

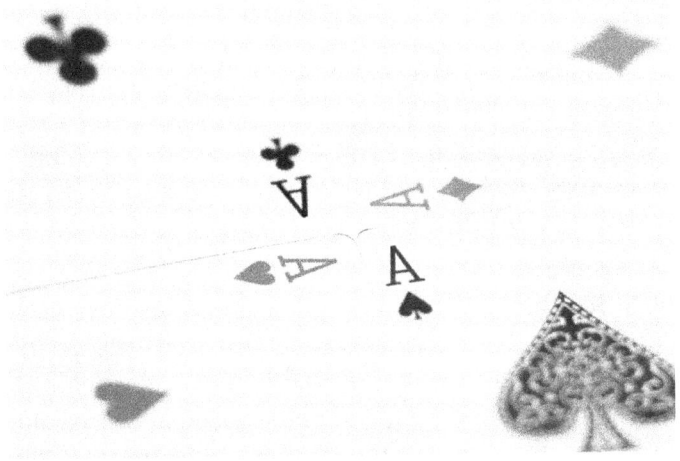

The four suits represent the four seasons in the year.[6]

The four suits represent the four seasons in a year. Hearts represent spring, which is when you experience new growth. Diamonds represent the abundance and prosperity of the summer, and Clubs are reminiscent of autumn when you reap what you've sown. Spades are winter, a time when everything hibernates and goes within.

These suits are also connected to the four classical elements. The Hearts are connected to watery emotions and the deep wells of intuition within you. Diamonds are of the earth, pregnant with resources and rich with treasures. Clubs are connected to flames of creativity and passion that burn in one and all, even though they are but embers in some and in others a raging inferno. As for Spades, they are airy cards that have to do with intellect, mental prowess, and communication.

The Hearts

The Hearts suit is also known as the Cups suit in Tarot. It's one of the four main suits you'll encounter in cartomancy, and it's all about matters of the heart, dreams, relationships, emotions, intuition, and the subconscious or unconscious. It's about the things that bubble beneath the surface of the deep. It is believed that the physical world isn't the only one, and it shares a connection with invisible realms, realms you'd consider spiritual or metaphysical. The archetypes and symbols on the Hearts suit are connected to those realms, possessing deep insight into what it means to be alive and evolve spiritually.

The Hearts suit is the suit that tells you everything about the relationships in your life and how they influence you. It tells you about your spiritual path and how you're doing with your self-exploration and discovery. The cards in this suit will reveal everything about your challenges and victories, and the things you have experienced or will experience that will change you for better or worse as you discover your authentic, spiritual self. This suit represents messages from your intuitive self and wisdom that wells up from the subconscious mind. It's about getting in touch with worlds unseen, following your instincts, feeling your gut on every issue, and trusting what it tells you.

Hearts are connected to the heart itself, which, as everyone knows, is the center of love, passion, hate, and other emotions. The heart is at the center of who you are. It's from your heart that your true desires are born and where you hold your true self, devoid of any of the ego's decorations, masks, and costumes. Therefore, The Heart suit is an invitation to your emotional world, asking you to dive deep and receive the valuable treasures in your heart's wisdom. Here's a quick look at what each card in this suit implies.

Ace of Hearts: Expect a new beginning in relationships and friendships. This could be a new lover, marriage, or something good happening to you. It represents the potential to develop powerful emotional ties with others.

2 of Hearts: This card represents the connection of two people as they become one in love. It's also asking you to spend some time with those you love. This card carries the energy of balance, connection, harmony, and partnership, representing the ideas of emotional cooperation and compatibility. It's asking you to demonstrate more understanding as you relate with others, which means being open to vulnerability and reconciliation.

3 of Hearts: When you draw this card, it indicates that you aren't very committed to a relationship, or at the very least, you feel indecisive about it. However, some interpret this more positively. As they say, it represents an abundant, joyful experience of love in every way possible.

4 of Hearts: Emotional stability and security are the energies that this card exudes. It tells you that you're in a committed partnership or marriage. When about home affairs, it implies that you're in a safe and nurturing environment. The 4 of Hearts is also about learning to set boundaries and ground your emotions to continue to enjoy the love that feels safe.

5 of Hearts: Drawing this card represents enormous changes that will affect your family and home life. These changes could be good or bad. Perhaps someone's getting divorced or moving to a new place. Either way, the status quo will be disrupted. The 5 of Hearts is the heartbreak card, representing grief, loss, release, and resilience when dealing with emotional turbulence.

6 of Hearts: Expect harmonious interactions with others, leading you to whatever you desire. This card is about freely giving and receiving love and letting kindness lead the way in your dealings with others. Its energy is forgiving and selfless.

7 of Hearts: This card can represent someone likely to disappoint you. Alternatively, it represents being introspective and searching your heart to discover your true feelings about someone or something.

8 of Hearts: Commitment, developing stronger bonds, and emotional changes are the messages this card carries. It's about sticking with someone or something for the long haul, being mature in expressing your emotions, choosing loyalty above anything else, and investing everything you can to develop and sustain loving connections in your life. Drawing this card means you'll be at an event that will give you the opportunity of a lifetime, romantically or financially.

9 of Hearts: This card tells you someone wants to take their relationship with you to greater heights. Perhaps they'd like to propose or start a family with you. Expect to experience satisfaction in your connections and love affairs.

10 of Hearts: Expect some good news. You'll learn of this at a party or someplace where many people are gathered. The card also represents family unity and being fulfilled emotionally in that context.

Jack of Hearts: This card represents your most trusted friend or lover. When you draw this along with the Queen of Hearts, it could represent a couple. On its own, it's someone creative, sensitive, and full of compassion. Usually, it represents a young person. This card also represents your insights from intuition and emotional development.

Queen of Hearts: This card represents your fantasy. It could also stand in for a female lover or someone pregnant. Marriage may also be on the horizon. This card's energy is nurturing, deep, and intuitive. It's the embodiment of femininity.

King of Hearts: The King of Hearts represents masculine energy and can stand in for a father figure. It's a man of influence who is in touch with his emotions and is sweet. This person demonstrates love in the context of leadership, balancing his authority with his emotions so that he tempers justice with kindness.

The Diamonds

Sometimes the Diamonds suit is called the Coins or Pentacles suit. This suit concerns practical affairs, money, material wealth, and the physical world. The Diamonds are about everything you own, your career, and what you do to advance in life. The Diamonds represent everything about manifestation and making your dreams come true. They show you all the practical things you must do to get where you need to go, how much effort will be required to make your goals happen, and whether you should keep treading the path you're on.

Diamonds demonstrate what you need to do to help you get in the flow of prosperity and abundance using practical skills that you possess and resources around you that you may have been blind to for a while. It's about your business and vocation and guidance on what to do to get the financial status you desire. It's about taking your dreams and making them real through action.

Esoterically, the Diamonds suit also has to do with your health. It's about how good you feel in your body and what you can do to take better care of it. The cards in this suit can show you the connection between your spiritual life and your health, so you know the importance of feeding yourself on both levels so you can be the best version of yourself.

Finally, this suit is about integrating your spiritual and physical lives. It's about ensuring that the things you hold in high esteem align with what you're experiencing in the observable, objective world to feel like you have a purpose and meaning in your life. These cards ask you to remember that your physical life should be a tool to help you develop spiritually. The Diamonds are connected to the diamond itself. This hard, durable thing represents strength, endurance, and resilience. Think about forming a diamond; you can draw parallels from that process to your life. To produce the precious stone, there's got to be some refinement, and this is the same with your life. You need to take the raw materials you've been given — your talents, skills, and natural inclinations — and make them work for you, and this is what Diamonds generally teach you when you draw them. Now, let's see what each card means in this suit.

Ace of Diamonds: Drawing this card means there's something important that you will learn about your business. It's a sign that there's potential for you to make something of yourself financially or that abundance is coming your way. The message here is that you should prepare yourself for financial prosperity and other opportunities for growth in a material sense, so you can experience stability in that aspect of life.

2 of Diamonds: When you spot this card, expect to receive some good news about your investments. The number two represents the idea of duality and balance, so drawing this card means you must find a balance between your material pursuits and spiritual growth. It implies that you should find balance in allocating and using your resources.

3 of Diamonds: The 3 of Diamonds card demonstrates some uncertainty regarding finances. If you're not careful, you may be caught in legal problems. Alternatively, this card represents manifesting your abundance at last, working with your practical skills, and improving your craft. This card tells you that you have talents you must develop and work hard at, as this is how you will gain the prosperity you seek.

4 of Diamonds: Drawing this card means you need to be more responsible with your finances to stay stable. It's about accumulating immense wealth through making sensible, smart choices and working hard on your goals.

5 of Diamonds: You should expect some sort of economic change. It could be good or bad, but whatever it is, it definitely requires preparation. You may have to contend with financial setbacks or have a sudden windfall. The best way to tell what it might be is within the context of other cards. Drawing this card implies you've got to be resourceful and creative in handling the situation.

6 of Diamonds: It's time to pay attention to your debts. Do your best to settle them. Also, look at your budget and adjust it or create one if you don't have one. You also should look into investing for your financial future. The 6 of Diamonds is also a card of generosity, blessings, giving, and receiving. It tells you that the more you give, the more you receive.

7 of Diamonds: Be mindful of what you do with your money, especially regarding investment. You must evaluate your options carefully before you make a decision. Be prudent about what you do with your resources. Think about where you're at financially before making a major decision or putting your money into something.

8 of Diamonds: Drawing this card is lovely because a great, unexpected windfall is just around the corner. The number 8 is reminiscent of the infinity sign, and you can expect a good amount of money that is impactful enough to feel like infinite abundance. Keep your eyes on the prize and stay dedicated to your goal, even if it seems impossible.

9 of Diamonds: This card tells you that you've attained or are close to attaining fulfillment in your financial endeavors. The number nine represents completions and endings; therefore, this card could also represent the idea of finishing a financial journey you've been on, having finally attained security. It's the card of the materialization of everything you've ever wanted to attain relative to your finances and business.

10 of Diamonds: You're drawing close to the very zenith of your accomplishments. You've worked hard and will now enjoy the fruits of your labor. You will be greatly rewarded for choosing the best, most balanced path to success.

Jack of Diamonds: This card represents someone full of ambition. This practical person diligently applies himself to his work, keeping his career goals within sight. This person could be male or female and is driven to get things started and succeed at entrepreneurship. This person is also young (usually). Some, however, say that the Jack of Diamonds represents someone bringing you bad financial news. You can tell which is the case by working within the context of the other cards you've drawn (or will draw) and the question being answered.

Queen of Diamonds: This represents a woman or feminine force with a love for parties and gossip. You may think of this card as someone who is abundant, practical, and has much wisdom to share with you when it comes to finances. The card is about being financially independent and prudent with your money so that you grow it even more.

King of Diamonds: This card can represent a businessman (or a businesswoman with masculine energy) who has found great power and success in his affairs. This person is in charge of wealth and is a responsible decision-maker. The card represents your power to create abundance for yourself, dominate finance, and manage your resources with great wisdom.

The Clubs

Sometimes, the Clubs suit is known as the Baton or Wands suit. Its energy is a representation of the fire of creativity and inspiration. This suit is connected to your growth, passion, and ambition. It is about starting new endeavors. It is about the spark of inspiration that you get to begin something new. Whenever you draw a card from the Club suit, it represents giving birth to new ideas and nurturing those ideas so that they blossom into their fullness.

The Club Suit is about discovering yourself and developing your spiritual awareness to the point where you can use it to influence your physical life. The cards you draw from this suit all offer guidance that aligns with your inspiration. In other words, all the wisdom you receive from these cards is rooted in spiritual principles that govern life.

The Clubs are all about your passion and determination to be a success. It is about expressing your highest calling as a leader and choosing the attitude of determination when you embark on any creative endeavor. Clubs carry the energy of taking charge in asserting your authentic self. Often, when people draw this card, they are required to express their inner strength when dealing with challenges in life.

The Club suit is also connected to intuition. It is about waking up your latent psychic abilities and using them following divine wisdom to bring you the spiritual insight and physical changes that you desire. Clubs ask you to trust the voice from within because it is the voice of truth and transformational passion. Therefore, the Club suit is all about alchemy, taking the raw material of the passion within you and converting that into the manifestation you seek. Now it's time to examine what each card in the Clubs' suit represents.

Ace of Clubs: This represents a desire to know everything you can. It can also represent a unique skill or talent that you alone possess. This card is the essence of fire. It is about the creative energy that you use for new ideas. Drawing this card means you're about to start something new along creative lines or spiritual lines about which you are passionate.

2 of Clubs: This card is about cooperation and blending your ideas with others. It is about acknowledging the creative forces within you and someone else and finding a way to bring them together that works. This card is also a reminder that you need to communicate clearly and sincerely with others and do your best not to get entangled in confrontations to avoid getting into a situation where you are disappointed.

3 of Clubs: When you draw this card, it represents either an extreme amount of creativity (which is a good thing) or the stress you must undergo in creating something. The three Clubs also represent the ideas of expansion and growth and the realization that you can create much more than you thought possible. When you draw this card, it asks you to look within and discover your skills and do your best to develop them. As you do this, opportunities will present themselves to you, allowing you to broaden your horizons and achieve much more than you thought possible. This card also asks you to be enthusiastic and optimistic about the new things that come your way and be willing to try things outside your comfort zone.

4 of Clubs: Find a way to ground your creative energy. In other words, you are meant to find practical outlets for that energy to convert potential into something real. The 4 of Clubs is about foundation, stability, and having a solid framework for your ideas. It is about going after your creative goals for the long term. Drawing this card also means that you must do your best to cultivate a stable sense of self and peace of mind to experience something amazing.

5 of Clubs: You need to change something about your life. It's a good time to discover new things. You may be pleasantly surprised to find you have an affinity for a sport or hobby you never thought you'd be interested in. Expect to contend with conflicts and challenges as you express yourself creatively. To overcome these challenges, you must be flexible and willing to change. Seek innovative ways to fix your problems. Being resilient and persevering through everything will help you.

6 of Clubs: This is a card of success and victory in your creative endeavors. You will be or are being recognized for all that you have achieved in the field of creativity. It results from all the work you have put into obtaining your goals and everyone finally recognizing your creative prowess. This card affirms that you are a creative powerhouse and must lean on your intuition to gain better things.

7 of Clubs: You feel stuck, trapped, or confined. This could be not just in your creative life but your romantic life. You need to take time to be introspective. Reflect on your life so far, and explore yourself – that is how you will grow. You must seek guidance from within and ensure that whatever creative projects you are involved in align with your true values.

8 of Clubs: The energy of this card is progress. It is about the momentum you experience as you work to accomplish your creative goals. You will manifest the visions you have held in your mind as you are driven toward success. Drawing this card means you must focus and stay determined as you pursue your dreams. Some readers say that this card is also a sign that you are struggling with confusion. They say it means you must be careful because you may experience major problems relating to others if you do not sort out your problem.

9 of Clubs: 9, the number of completion, implies that this card is about finishing a phase or project. You have finally achieved the dreams that you sought. The satisfaction that you have sought for the longest time is now yours.

10 of Clubs: This card says you will be traveling soon. Your travels are essential to your creative endeavors. Therefore, do not be tempted to pass on an opportunity to go somewhere new. This card also represents blending what you know and have experienced to apply that to your creative work.

Jack of Clubs: The Jack of Clubs is someone you can trust. This is an honest person who makes a point of telling you everything that you must know. This person may be a close friend of yours.

Queen of Clubs: The Queen of Clubs is a woman full of charisma. She is in a position of power. She can help you with whatever you seek to learn or accomplish.

King of Clubs: This represents a man who never compromises when it comes to his integrity. This man is an excellent person to have by your side as a friend because he constantly proves himself to be loyal and generous.

The Spades

The Spades suit is also known as the Swords suit. This suit is all about obstacles and difficulties you must face. Very often, the suit is considered a negative one. It usually is about having to make very difficult choices and decisions in life about major things.

The Spades suit is about communication, sharing ideas, and intellect. It is connected to the idea of being rational and working with the power of your mind. The sword is often seen as a symbol representing discernment in making decisions. You can use it to cut through confusing clouded thoughts, so you can get to the heart and truth of the matter.

The cards in this suit are meant to help you to figure out the difference between what is real and what only appears to be real. Drawing cards from this suit will help you make informed decisions based on solid facts. This suit is also related to the power in your tongue, in the sense that you can give life or kill, depending on the words you choose when interacting with others. The Spades can help you figure out how to deal with sensitive issues and express yourself so that you deliver the truth without severely damaging someone.

Another thing about the Spades suit is that it will help you discover the limiting beliefs holding you back from achieving your highest ideals. If you know that you can stomach the truth about yourself, you will not shy away from any reading with a Spade in it. You will understand the power you can use for your benefit as it can help you to transmute conflicts and challenges into opportunities to improve in every way possible. Now that you understand what the Spades suit is all about, it is time to talk about the individual cards in this suit.

Ace of Spades: You will deal with major changes in your life. Something you've grown accustomed to will have to end to make room for the new. This card represents the fact that your mind has infinite potential and intellect.

2 of Spades: You're going to encounter a difficult situation. If improperly handled, this may lead you and a loved one to part ways. You must carefully consider your choices now, considering various viewpoints in order to make a balanced decision.

3 of Spades: You will be sad due to something stressful. You may receive terrible news. There's also a possibility that your job security may be threatened. Or, you may be dealing with fear and indecision regarding a certain matter. The Three of Spades is also about expanding your mind through learning, discovering the skills that you have within you, and following through on your ideas to see where they lead.

4 of Spades: You should expect your health or career to become stable soon. The tough times that you have been contending with or about to come to an end. This card is the energy of stability and organization regarding your intellectual pursuits. It asks you to be disciplined in your affairs.

5 of Spades: Very soon, you will have to walk away from something with which you have grown familiar. You may be leaving your job for a new one or relocating to a new home. You may also be dealing with the end of your romantic relationship. The 5 of Spades is a card that embodies the conflicts you must deal with in your mind when facing adversity. The card tells you that the storm is the opportunity for you to grow and become something more by tapping into your inner resilience.

6 of Spades: Expect to be rocked in your career or finances. This card also represents the path you must take from your present confused state to clarity. This card calls you out of your limited thinking to more expansive ideas.

7 of Spades: Soon, you may have to contend with losing someone important due to disagreements or other issues. In addition, the 7 of Spades ask you to look within yourself and question your beliefs to expand beyond the cage in which they have trapped you. This is a card of self-awareness.

8 of Spades: You may have to struggle with challenges at work. These challenges will force you to come to a point where you must make a critical decision about what to do next. This is the card of mental fortitude and determination. You will make your way through this obstacle one way or another.

9 of Spades: You may experience a loss due to death. This card also asks you to do what you must to set yourself free of negative thought patterns to end your life's current phase of hardship and move on to something newer and better.

10 of Spades: You will struggle with grief and worry. This could be because you're struggling with health issues or the aftermath of bad news.

You may also find that you are gripped by fear. It is important to understand that this is temporary.

Jack of Spades: This individual is extremely negative. If you are not careful, they will stab you in the back. They are also holding you back from accomplishing what you need to. Therefore, taking a critical look at the people in your life to pinpoint the toxic person and get rid of them as soon as possible is important.

Queen of Spades: This woman is an expert at manipulating others to get what she wants. Often, the results of her manipulation do not benefit anyone else besides her. You must beware of this character because she is extremely cruel and is constantly on the lookout to display her malevolence toward anyone within her sight.

King of Spades: This individual is a man who has authority and is in the habit of causing trouble wherever he is. You need to beware of this character because he will cause you trouble, particularly regarding your relationship.

Now that you understand what each card implies, you can also check in with your intuition to see what else you pick up on during a reading from the card. Remember that these are only guidelines and that their meanings can change drastically depending on the context in which the cards appear. The next chapter will reveal all you need to learn about spreads and layouts that you can use in cartomancy.

Chapter 4: Spreads and Layouts

In this chapter, you'll learn that there are various cartomancy methods. Ultimately, you're the one who gets to decide the technique and specific deck of cards to be used. In this chapter, you will learn about the most common, basic spreads and, later, the more complex ones.

The Basic Spreads

The following spreads are the most common ones and worth looking into before you dive into the more complex stuff.

The One-Card Draw

One-card draw.[7]

This is one of the easiest draws you can use in your practice. All you have to do is draw one card out of the deck to respond to a specific question or gain insight into a particular problem you're dealing with. The beauty of this draw is that it is beginner-friendly, and you can gain profound insights from just one card.

To perform a one-card draw, you must first enter a meditative state by quieting your mind. Then, shuffle the deck while keeping your intention or question in mind. As you shuffle, you will get an intuitive nudge when it's time to stop and pick a card from the deck.

Once you've drawn the card, it's time to interpret its meaning. This means you need to pause to look at the card's colors, pictures, and any symbols it may have. You must understand that every card possesses a unique story seeking interpretation through the medium of your intuition. Therefore, you should take your time with this and not be in a hurry to say something. If you have trouble understanding what the card is trying to tell you, do not be afraid to draw another card (though this would not be the one-card draw when you do so).

One of the major advantages of working with this one-card draw is that it is simple enough to establish a deep connection to the cards you draw. When you are focused on just one card, it becomes easier for you to learn to work with your intuition and better interpret the meaning of each card presented, depending on the context. The one-card draw is the best option when you don't have enough time or are in a hurry.

As great as this draw is, you must realize that it does not offer a broad enough perspective on your question or situation compared to the more complex spreads. This is because you glean information from just one card rather than several. However, this doesn't mean you should snub the one-card draw method, as it can still give you the most profound answers.

The Three-Card Spread

The three-card spread."

As you've already gathered from the name of the spread, the three-card spread is one where you draw three cards out of the deck and set them up in a specific pattern to indicate certain things. There are several iterations of the three-card spread. Let's take a look at each one.

Past — Present — Future: This is a classic method of working with a three-card spread that lets you know the circumstances and influences surrounding your current location. The first card is your past and lets you know how you got to where you are. The second card represents your present and demonstrates exactly what you face regarding challenges and opportunities. The final card shows you what the future could hold. It allows you to see possible outcomes if you continue your path.

Mind — Body — Spirit: This spread will show you what's happening within yourself on different levels. The first card drawn represents your mind. It's meant to show you the thoughts that you have consciously and beneath the surface, what you believe in, and your academic goals. The second card is representative of your body. This card shows you the state of your health and well-being and other important information about your physical self. The final card drawn represents your spirit, giving you insights into the path you walk spiritually, how you can grow, and how you can rely on your intuition to become an evolved being.

Problem — Action — Outcome: Working with this technique, the first card represents the obstacle or problem you're dealing with. It shows you its true source so that you can address it at its core. The next card is the action you should take to fix whatever is broken. The last card is the result or outcome you should expect if you follow the recommended action path.

The great thing about the three-card spread is that it's also a simple one for beginners. Better than the one-card draw, this method gives you a more comprehensive understanding of the question. Working with elements such as your past, present, and future gives you a deep, holistic perspective of your present situation. This implies that you can make choices from enough data based on truth, and you will feel more comfortable and confident in pursuing your path.

As great as a three-card spread is, it does have some limitations. For instance, this card spread may not be adequate for digging into the complex, intricate nature of certain circumstances where you may need more insight. It offers a snapshot of things rather than getting heavily into the situation. Another thing you need to be aware of: the meaning of each card may be taken out of context if you do not consider the three cards as a unit. Therefore, you need to consider how each card interacts with the others before you offer your reading.

The Celtic Cross Spread

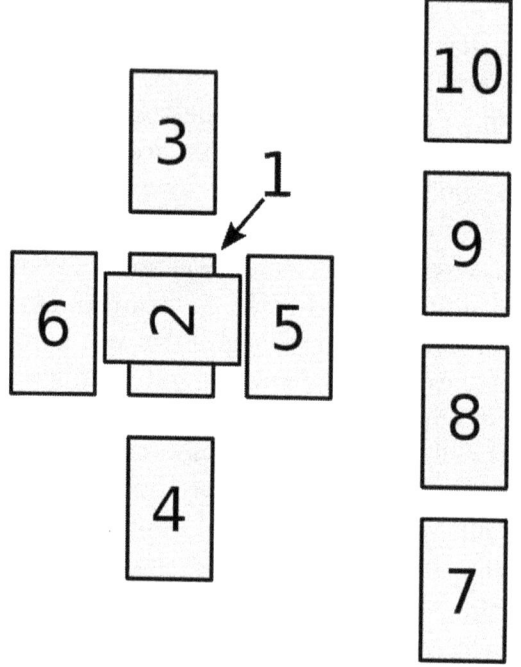

The Celtic cross spread.[9]

The Celtic cross spread is an interesting spread with 10 cards set up to form a cross and staff. The first known mention of the Celtic cross spread was in 1910 by A. E. Waite in the introduction to A Pictorial Key to the Tarot. Waite was part of the Hermetic Order of the Golden Dawn, which often used this specific spread. There are various ways to do the Celtic cross spread.

The Traditional Celtic Cross: With this spread, 10 cards are set out in the cross pattern. The first card represents the issue on which you want clarity. It talks about the main theme of the question being posed. The second card represents the forces that influence the situation you are contending with and the challenges you must face. The third card is your subconscious mind, and it's meant to help you learn the underlying factors in that situation and the hidden motivations of all the players involved. The fourth card represents your very recent past. It tells you all you need to know about what led you to where you are.

The fifth card represents a possible future result or the energies coming into play. The sixth card is your immediate future and offers information about what to expect in the coming days or weeks. The seventh card represents you. It shows you your attitude towards the circumstance you're faced with and how you are addressing it. The eighth card is representative of the external forces like events and people that will have a part to play in the final outcome. The 9th card sheds light on your dreams, fears, and hopes. It helps you understand what's going on with you emotionally. The final card is the ultimate resolution or result of the situation.

The Modified Celtic Cross: This version differs from the traditional one in that extra cards help you gain more insight into the situation. It starts as the traditional spread, but after those 10 classic cards, you can draw more cards to place in certain positions to gain more information or clarity on those aspects. For instance, you may want more information on the fifth card to understand the possible outcomes of the problem you're dealing with and be better prepared to handle them, so you can draw another card from the deck to clarify that fifth one. The great thing about these extra cards is that they make your reading more nuanced and in-depth, providing a more satisfactory answer you can act on confidently.

The wonderful thing about the Celtic cross spread, whether the traditional or modified version, is that you can use it to not just look at your past, present, and future but to understand everything that's going on, on a conscious and subconscious level. It's a flexible cartomancy spread because it can address all aspects of your life, like personal growth, love life, finances, etc. When you lay out all the cards in a Celtic cross spread, you are presented with the smorgasbord of symbolism that provides a much richer, layered, detailed interpretation of events.

As great as this spread is, it does have certain drawbacks. For one thing, it may be too complex for some people. It does require an in-depth understanding of the interplay between cards and how their meanings affect one another. So, as a new practitioner of cartomancy, you need to grasp what each card means and get familiar with how these meanings can influence one another before you begin working with this spread. You will encounter challenges when it comes to interpreting the cards. Still, if you choose to be patient, work with your intuition, and continue to practice, you will find yourself getting more adept at working with the Celtic cross spread.

The Grand Tableau

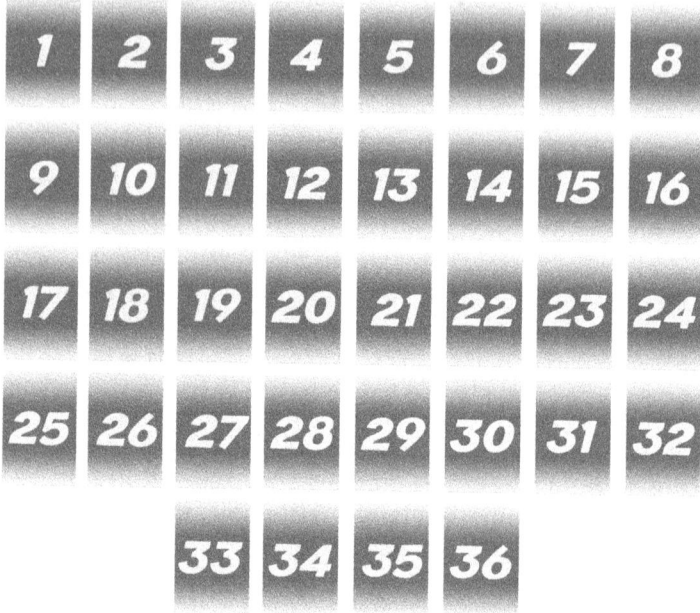

Grand Tableau Layout

Using all 36 cards in the deck, lay out the cards in the order shown above
4 rows of 8 cards
1 row of 4 cards

The Grand Tableau spread

The Grand Tableau is a spread that requires the Lenormand deck. Grand Tableau is French, meaning "big picture." The lovely thing about the spread is that it'll give you a panoramic view of everything in your life, from the past to your present and future. There are various ways that you can use the Grand Tableau spread.

The Traditional Grand Tableau: In this spread, you will lay 36 cards in a particular pattern to form a grid. Every card has its position that stands for the various aspects of your life or the question you're asking. Usually, the layout has various rows and columns, and they all intersect to create new meaning. The various positions can have different meanings depending on the system of interpretation that you follow.

The Focused Question Grand Tableau: This variation of the Grand Tableau spread focuses on just one area of your life or one question. You work with all 36 cards. However, the advantage of this version of the

Grand Tableau is that it will allow you to concentrate on the cards specifically connected to your inquiry. When you pay specific attention to the intersections or key spots tied to your question, you can gain profound wisdom about that area of your life.

The Grand Tableau is another spread offering you a deep, comprehensive insight into your situation. The level of nuance and detail you can attain with this spread is amazing and very useful. This is also an excellent spread for forecasting your possible future. Of course, this is not without its drawbacks, as it is a rather complex spread, and it requires a lot of time and focus to interpret this correctly.

The Tree of Life Spread

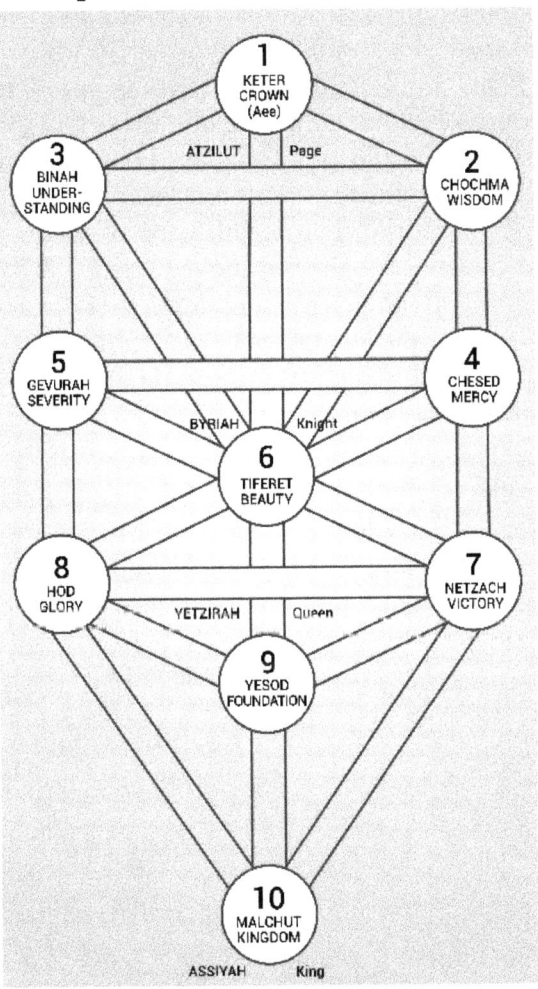

The Tree of Life spread.

This spread is rooted in ancient Kabbalistic wisdom. It is inspired by the Tree of Life in the Kabbalah. There are various ways you can use the spread.

The Traditional Tree of Life Spread: The cards are set out to mimic the Tree of Life in the Kabbalah. There are 10 positions in this layout, each representing one emanation or sephira on the tree. The cards are laid down from top to bottom, and each emanation connects to a specific aspect of life. The first card addresses spirituality and represents what you believe in and practice in your spiritual life and your connection to the divine. The next card is the persona card, which gives insight into how you appear in other people's eyes. The next card is the subconscious card. This card will expose what you truly feel, desire, and think beneath the surface. After this card is the home and family card, which shows you what life is like with your family members. The next one demonstrates your connection to your ancestors, as well as the history of your family. The sixth card represents how your past has played out and how it affects your present reality. The seventh card demonstrates your connection to other realms, like the spirit world. The eighth card of wisdom shows all the insights you have gained through your life experience. The ninth card is a card that shows how you have grown and developed or how you will do so in the future. The final card is the outcome card that demonstrates the likely results of the circumstance you are dealing with if you continue on the path of action you have chosen.

The Modified Tree of Life Spread: This spread has been modified in such a way as to offer more flexibility in the reading of the cards. You may assign certain areas of your life to specific positions on the Tree of Life that tie into the matter about which you are asking questions. You could pay attention only to matters involving your career, love life, or anything else.

The Romany Spread

The Romany spread

This spread requires 21 cards set up in three rows with seven cards per row. It is also known as the Gypsy spread.

The Traditional Romany Spread: Each row represents an aspect of your existence in this spread. The first represents the past, the second represents the present, and the last represents the future. The cards are read sequentially to gain insight into all the influences affecting your life.

The Modified Romany Spread: This one is similar to the traditional one, except you can customize it to your needs. For instance, you may add cards or remove cards. You can add extra rows if they serve your purpose or adjust the layout so that you only focus on specific aspects of life that may not necessarily correlate to the traditional past, present, or future setup.

Now that you understand the various spreads and layouts that you can use in cartomancy, the question is, how do you accurately interpret combined cards? Also, what does it mean when a card shows up reversed? You will discover the answers to these questions in the following chapter.

Chapter 5: Combinations and Reversed Cards

When reading multiple cards, it is important to understand that they will always influence the overall meaning you get from your reading. This is because the energies of the cards interact with one another in unique ways, varying from context to context. In this chapter, you'll learn how to interpret multiple cards that show up in a layout or spread and understand the reversed cards that definitely will turn up.

Patterns can be found when reading multiple cards.[10]

Finding Patterns

Seeking patterns in the various combinations of cards you draw can add more dimension and depth to your readings. It's common to look for patterns in pairs, trios, or quartets, so you can discover the underlying connections and other hidden meanings that aren't immediately easy to glean.

Pairs: The first pattern to consider is known as the pair. This is when you have two cards with similar numbers or suits showing up with each other side by side. Following are some keyword interpretations of the various pairs you may encounter. Still, please note that you should also work with your intuition because that could offer something more nuanced in your interpretations or even different from what you have read in this book.

- **Pair of Aces:** Reconnection
- **Pair of Kings:** Helpful advice
- **Pair of Queens:** Expressing curiosity
- **Pair of Jacks:** Having discussions
- **Pair of Tens:** New luck
- **Pair of Nines:** Upcoming contentment and satisfaction
- **Pair of Eights:** Instability
- **Pair of Sevens:** Love shared
- **Pair of Sixes:** Contrasts and differences
- **Pair of Fives:** Insecurity
- **Pair of Fours:** Small opportunities
- **Pair of Threes:** Making choices
- **Pair of Twos:** Separation

Pair of Jokers: Anything can happen **Trios:** These patterns show up in threes. The following are the interpretations of each trio:

- **Trio of Aces:** Harmony and balance
- **Trio of Kings:** Excellent support
- **Trio of Queens:** Gossip
- **Trio of Jacks:** Quarrelsome energy

- **Trio of Tens**: Recompense
- **Trio of Nines:** Success
- **Trio of Eights:** Lightened load
- **Trio of Sevens:** Accomplishment and fulfillment
- **Trio of Sixes:** Dedication and hard work
- **Trio of Fives:** Satisfaction
- **Trio of Fours**: High odds of success
- **Trio of Threes:** Balance and stability
- **Trio of Twos:** Switching lanes

Quartets: There are four suits, so naturally, you can expect interesting quartets to show up in readings occasionally. Here are keyword interpretations of quartets to guide you:

- **Quartet of Aces**: Victory
- **Quartet of Kings:** Success, acknowledgment, and honor
- **Quartet of Queens:** Scandalous events
- **Quartet of Jacks**: Fighting and battling
- **Quartet of Tens:** Better changes
- **Quartet of Nines**: Sudden windfall and unexpected, good news
- **Quartet of Eights:** Worry and concern
- **Quartet of Sevens:** Sameness
- **Quartet of Sixes:** Sudden difficulties and curveballs
- **Quartet of Fives:** Joy and happiness
- **Quartet of Fours:** 50-50 odds
- **Quartet of Threes**: Optimism and hope
- **Quartet of Twos:** Being at an intersection, crossroads, and choices

Considering the Numbers

When interpreting drawn cards, you should consider what the numbers mean, as they will add more depth to the meaning you glean from them. Every number has unique energy and meaning, bringing you greater clarity when you understand them. You can also look at the numbers from the context of numerology, which is the study of the influence of numbers on everyone and every aspect of everyday life. Some cartomancers will assign each number two meanings, which are opposite. The positive meaning is applied when the number appears in a red suit. The negative interpretation is used instead if it's in the black suit. With that said, here's a look at the meanings of each number when working with this system:

- 1 — Beginning or ending; starting or finishing
- 2 — Working together or working against each other
- 3 — Increasing or reducing; expanding or contracting
- 4 — Stability or instability; balance or imbalance
- 5 — Action or rest
- 6 — Communication or silence; knowledge or ignorance
- 7 — Improving or regressing
- 8 — Health or illness; healing or deteriorating health
- 9 — Dreams or disappointments
- 10 — Victory or defeat; success or failure
- 11 (the Jack) — Thinking or speaking
- 12 (the Queen) — External guidance or internal wisdom
- 13 (the King) — Leading or following

Key Positions

As you look at the spread, you should pay attention to the positions of the cards, particularly the ones in the corners or the center. These cards are like foundations to your reading; their meaning will offer you deep insight that shapes the answers the reader seeks. The middle card is like the heart of your reading, demonstrating the main essence of the question. You cannot ignore this card because it represents everything happening here and now, which spreads its influence like tentacles into the future. When considering the cards in the middle, you should ask yourself questions. For instance, what does a card in the middle show you about the current situation in which you seek clarity? What's the connection of the middle card to the challenge you're facing or the main goal you want to accomplish? What message does this card convey regarding the most important aspects of your life? By looking at the card in the middle, focusing on it, and allowing your intuition to speak to you about it, you will develop a deep insight into the forces responsible for your destiny.

You must also consider the cards that show up at the corners. Usually, the corner cards are very important. Within these cards, you will find the keys to hidden doors in the subconscious that help to explain exactly what the seeker is going through and their deepest desires.

It is also important for you to consider the relationship between the cards as you read them. You will learn so many secrets by considering how close they are or how far apart and the alignments they share. For instance, when you have cards that face each other across your spread, these cards may act as mirrors to each other, representing opposing energies that seek balance. However, you notice that certain cards appear to oppose each other. In that case, you must ask yourself what that implies for your query. Sometimes, the cards will form a bridge between other cards. These cards are easy to pick out because you'll notice the same suit or number creating this bridge. It is important to pay attention to these things because they will show you how various elements dance with one another to create the show that is your life. They will offer much more minute detail than just considering individual cards independently.

As you observe your spread, you may realize that certain cards appear more prominent than others, drawing your eye. It appears as though their energy is literally screaming at you for attention. One of the ways to notice these cards is through their size or how closely placed they are to the center. You may also give significance to the cards based on their connection to the question that you were asking. Make a point of getting in touch with your intuition before doing the reading. You may feel the energetic, emotional pull of a card. It is important to pay attention to any card that draws your eye and allow it to dictate the main themes of the reading.

Elemental Associations

Another way you can glean meaning from the card is by considering the primal elements the cards and suits possess. By considering the interplay of the various elements that show up, you will understand the dynamics of the various cards and how they affect one another to give you an on-point reading.

As you already know, each suit has its own element. You can return to Chapter 3 to refresh your memory about each suit. When you understand the elemental energies contained in its suit, you can then take that information and use it to figure out what the various suit combinations in your reading may imply. For instance, when you notice that you have different suits acting in alignment, which suggests that the elements complement each other. For instance, you get Heart and Diamond cards in your reading. The Hearts are emotional cards, and the Diamonds are practical cards, and merging these two could indicate financial stability and consideration for your feelings while getting financial freedom.

It is also possible to have a clash of energies between the cards. For instance, the Club is a card that suggests fire and ambition. If you draw that card along with a Spade, which suggests being introspective, it could be a sign that you are having trouble finding the sweet spot between taking action and thinking something over. This means you have to find a way to balance these things.

Sometimes, you will discover that one suit appears to dominate your entire reading. This tells you that elemental energy is predominant in your life. Considering this, you can uncover clues that help you understand your life's work and theme. For instance, discovering that your reading is rife with Diamonds could mean you are heavily focused on the material side of life.

Another noteworthy thing you must consider is how balanced or imbalanced the reading is regarding elemental energy. For instance, when reading is properly balanced, it will have enough representation from all four suits, which tells you that your life is in harmony and that there is balance in your spiritual, material, emotional, and intellectual life. It suggests that you are very flexible when it comes to the way you approach your life. However, in the previously mentioned situation where only one suit predominates your reading, it indicates that you have not been paying attention to other equally important aspects of your life. For instance, in the previous example, you may have been sacrificing your health, love life, and other things on the altar of your financial aspirations.

Reversals

Sometimes when you're reading, you will encounter reversed cards. These cards are not to be ignored because they are extremely powerful, showing you parts of your psyche that may have been hidden or the aspects of your life that you have neglected. These cards show up as a disruption of energy flow. They are reversed because they draw your attention, acting as a clarion call to finally face the obstacles and challenges you have refused to because sticking your head in the sand felt more comfortable. Reverse cards require you to be *comfortable with being uncomfortable*. That's what it'll take to overcome your obstacles and grow and learn from them.

Reversals bring in contrasting energies. These energies are meant to make the reading even more accurate. When cards are upright, this tells you that the energy is free-flowing and that you continue to move forward, building momentum as you do in whatever endeavor you're concerned with. However, a reversed card appears as a challenge to stand against the status quo. Think of it as the representation of delays, the setbacks you deal with, and the conflicts you face on the inside, which no one else knows about. Therefore, you need to look closely at reversed cards when they appear because they have a lot of wisdom you can act on to take your life where you need to go.

Reversed cards will show you the obstacles you've been contending with, even if you have not been willing to look at them because you've been afraid. It is important that when everything is against you, you choose to be unrelenting in your pursuits. You must remain resilient to discover strength you did not know you possessed. This is the gift that reversed cards offer you in a reading.

Another great thing about these cards is that they can demonstrate your life's subconscious, hidden parts. Everyone has a shadow. It doesn't matter what you do to maintain a sunny disposition or how hard you work to always appear nice. Everyone has an aspect of himself that he would prefer to remain hidden in the dark. However, reversed cards force you to plumb the depths of your unconscious mind and finally face your demons. When your demons have been revealed, the good news is you will become much more aware of who you are and what you're capable of, and you will be able to transmute the darkness to light.

The reversed card forces you to come face to face with the truth. In other words, it acts as an obliterator of illusions. It will destroy the lies you have been telling yourself for the longest time. It will also expose other people's true intentions towards you, depending on whether that is the focus of your reading.

Interpreting Reversed Cards

Here are some tips for interpreting reversed cards in the context of other cards:

1. Pay attention to opposing energies in the form of upright counterparts to the reversed cards. For instance, say you noticed an upright King of Diamonds and the reversed Ace of Hearts next to each other. This could demonstrate that you are finding many conflicts between your financial pursuits and your emotional satisfaction.
2. Consider the delays and obstacles you face and whatever area of life you ask the cards about. You must consider the cards surrounding the reversed card because those cards indicate aspects of your life that will be affected by the reversed card's energies. For instance, pulling a 7 of Hearts and a reversed 5 of Spades strongly indicates that you must deal with many more setbacks to achieve your goals.
3. Pay attention to any lingering issues that are yet to be resolved. Sometimes reversed cards are about unfinished business. To determine if this is the case, consider the patterns between reversed cards and the others in the spread. Say you have a reversed 10 of Clubs and the reversed Queen of Diamonds. This could suggest that you're struggling in your career and finances and must pay attention to them, or things will worsen.
4. You should also consider that the reversed cards represent energies hidden within you. They point to the various fears, hidden emotions, and aspects of yourself which you have refused to acknowledge are real. To understand the hidden interplay of the various energies within you, you must look at the cards surrounding the reversed card. An upright Ace of Clubs next to a reversed 9 of Hearts may mean you have continued suppressing your emotional needs or must look at everything about your creativity and passion.

When a Reversed Card Negates an Upright One

It is important to identify when a reversed card simply provides more context versus when it negates outright what an upright card implies. You can figure this out by noticing each card's visual direction in your spread. A card between an upright card and a reversed card shows that while the middle card is affected by the upright card to a degree, the reversed card resists that influence. For instance, assume you have a Queen of Hearts between a King of Hearts and a reversed 8 of Clubs. The King of Hearts is a warm card representing a generous person or someone in touch with their emotions, complementing the Queen of Hearts, which indicates success and influence. On the other hand, the reversed 8 of Clubs shows you that there are challenges regarding your ambitions or your material resources and the possible success coming your way. In this situation, the reversed 8 of Clubs opposes the King of Hearts' influence on the Queen of Hearts.

You must pay attention to the contrast in the symbolism between the reversed card and any upright card that appears energetically or visually connected. When the reversed card has qualities directly the opposite of the upright card, this is a clear sign of negation of the upright card.

Regardless of your preferred method of divining with the cards, you must understand that intuition is key. You cannot rely on your intellect, laws, or memory of each card's meaning. You must tap into the strong voice of your intuition to be properly guided through the otherwise confusing maze of card combinations. To develop this intuition, you must accept and trust what it gives you. The more you trust it, the clearer you'll perceive it, and the more accurate your readings will be in time. It also means spending a significant amount of time with the cards so that you can understand the language they speak to you and sense their energies.

Sample Combinations

Here are a few card combinations and potential interpretations you may draw from them:

Ace of Spades and Seven of Hearts: This could imply the start of something that profoundly changes you or your circumstances (the Ace of Spades) in a way that involves disappointment, or you need to retreat within to gain insight (Seven of Hearts).

Ten of Diamonds and Queen of Clubs: You will experience abundance in your finances (Ten of Diamonds) by being confident, making you charming in your ways (Queen of Clubs), and naturally drawing those people and situations you need to perpetuate said success.

King of Hearts, Ace of Diamonds, and Two of Spades: This refers to someone who is deeply compassionate and giving (King of Hearts) who is likely to bring you great opportunities for success (Ace of Diamonds), even though at the beginning of your connection there will be challenges to overcome (Two of Spades).

Jack of Clubs, Eight of Hearts, and Three of Diamonds: Drawing this combo suggests that there is a youthful person full of ambition (Jack of

Clubs) who will find joy (Eight of Hearts) by finally attaining stability in her finances through practical choices (Three of Diamonds).

Five of Spades, Nine of Clubs, Queen of Diamonds, and King of Spades: You will experience a time of change (Five of Spades), and by the time you're on the other side, you will have come into leadership and success, having finished your project or task (Nine of Clubs), and done your best to be wise about your investments (Queen of Diamonds). However, you must be careful not to use your newfound success to cause others heartache or unnecessary trouble (King of Spades).

So, you now know how to understand what a combination of drawn cards tells you and how you can draw meaning from them. How do you actually perform a reading? The next chapter will explain the process.

Chapter 6: Performing a Reading

Cartomancy readings should be approached with the right attitude and adequate preparation. This chapter will show you everything you need to do to give the best reading you can with zero sweat.

Creating Your Sacred Space

The first thing you must do before a cartomancy reading is to create a sacred space. Sacred spaces are important because, for one thing, they will help you with your focus. This craft requires concentration; you cannot afford to be distracted or struggle to get messages in a place full of conflicting energies that may distort the meanings you glean from the cards. When you create a sacred space, you dedicate an area to your practice that allows you to focus on your intuition and be present in the moment.

Sacred spaces are also important because you will conduct rituals and work with powerful imagery. This fact implies that your psychological state will shift in a way that makes it more conducive to receiving messages from intuition and spirits. Sacred spaces help you root your intentions firmly in your mind and create an atmosphere of divinity.

Creating a sacred space also entails preparing energetically and emotionally for your reading. It means you can let go of all distractions and worries, making receiving messages from the cards easier. The sacred space also acts as an energetic and physical boundary that keeps the profane from the profound. This is how to create your sacred space:

Performing your readings in a sacred space can help you work with powerful imagery.[11]

First, choose somewhere quiet and comfortable. Remember, you want *zero distractions.* The space could be in your home or in a nice spot outside.

Next, clear the space. If there's any form of clutter, you should get rid of it because it will likely add to your distractions. Removing the clutter encourages peace of mind and a sense of calmness, making connecting with the cards easier.

Set up the lighting. Lighting is important when you are creating your sacred space. Soft lamps or candles can create a gentle and welcoming atmosphere. Usually, it's best to go with natural light or something warm that allows you to really relax.

Use incense. You can make use of different aromas to affect your mood for the better. Therefore, invest in scented candles, incense sticks, or essential oils for your ritual space. Choose scents that make you feel present and relaxed, making it easier to connect your intuition.

Incorporate music. Music can also affect your mood and set you in a more receptive, open space in your mind. So, consider playing some ambient music that will make the atmosphere feel even more sacred than it does. You could also opt for nature sounds or work with meditation tracks that will allow you to relax.

Now it's time to create your altar. This is an optional step. However, you can create an altar if you feel you must. You can put meaningful images, symbols, crystals, and the cards you will work with on this altar. The altar aims to act as an anchor point where all your attention will be channeled during your readings.

Practicing Meditation

If you want to practice cartomancy, making meditation a daily habit is beneficial. Meditation will help you quiet your mind – which is essential for getting in touch with your intuition. There is no way you can experience the sense of calm needed for an accurate reading if your mind is constantly bothered by stressful thoughts, whether chatter or some distraction, making it tough to connect with your inner wisdom. By meditating, you put yourself in the right state of mind and receive messages from the cards and spirit.

Another important thing is that meditation helps you with your concentration. By meditating regularly, you can maintain your focus on basically any task for as long as you need. This skill is essential when it comes to cartomancy. Because the more concentrated you are on the task, the easier it'll be for you to glean the various meanings, symbolisms, and subtle nuances from the cards as you read.

Meditation is also a powerful way to develop your intuition. When you habitually turn within, you'll find a sure voice that lets you know what you need to know at every point. Everyone has intuition, but not everyone develops it. Consider meditating every day to have the level of connection necessary with your intuition to serve your readings.

Not only does meditation help you think clearly, it will also assist you with sensing energies. As you already know, every card has energy, and you'll be better at sensing it when you have the necessary tools. Meditation will give you heightened awareness, making picking up on subtle energies easy. You'll get such nuanced readings that anyone else working only with the meanings on the card couldn't possibly dream of. You can use two basic meditation methods to improve your cartomancy.

Mindfulness: With this meditation method, you only have to observe the thoughts, feelings, and sensations that you experience without offering any judgment. This is an excellent way to ensure you are always present during your readings. To practice mindfulness, sit in a comfortable position and ensure that you wear comfortable clothing. Ideally, you should be in a space that is free from distractions. If you live with other people, tell them not to bother you for the next 10 to 15 minutes. Sit, shut your eyes, part your lips slightly, inhale through your nose, and then exhale through your lips. As you breathe, pay attention to the breath. Notice how you feel when you inhale and exhale. You may notice that the exhale is longer than the inhale. This is fine. You'll also discover that your mind wanders away from the breath. This is not something to be upset about. In fact, you should be excited about noticing that your mind has wandered. When this happens, gently and lovingly acknowledge that you have been distracted and return your attention to your breath. Do this as often as you need to. The more you do this, the better you'll get at being mindful. Make this a daily practice, and you will see phenomenal results.

Visualization: This method of meditation involves using your imagination to create pictures in your mind. With this methodology, you will find it easier to connect with the pictures on the cards and their colors and what they symbolize on a much deeper level. To practice visualization, once more, find somewhere that is quiet and distraction-free. Shut your eyes, part your lips, inhale through your nose, and exhale through your mouth. Continue to do this until you feel your body relaxing and your mind getting stiller.

Next, picture yourself somewhere peaceful and calm; this could be a beach, a garden, or a mountaintop – whatever works for you is fine. Now, imagine that you're looking at a card. See the card in detail, taking note of all its symbols, colors, and the tiny little details that make that card unique from the others. Get so deep into your visualization that you begin to sense the energies of the cards as you watch them. By doing this every day, you become even better at connecting with the cards and a visual level and gleaning more accurate information from them.

You must remember that you cannot do meditation once and expect the effects to last forever. That would be akin to taking a shower once and assuming you will smell like roses for the rest of your life; meditation is not a fad but a way of life. And it is essential if you are going to practice cartomancy successfully.

Setting Intentions

Setting intentions is important when preparing for reading because this is how you clarify your purpose. This is how you focus your energy to ensure the reading stays on track. To set an intention properly, first, you must figure out why you're conducting a reading to begin with.

Take a moment to think about it. Is there a certain circumstance that you want more clarity on? Are you looking for validation? Do you just want more information on a certain person or aspect of your life? By grasping the motivation for seeking a reading, you will develop a strong intention, and you will guide the cards to give you more accurate answers.

When you figure out why you want to read, the next step is clarifying your intentions and goals. You need to ask yourself what it is you want from the cards. For instance, you may want very specific answers or prefer broad strokes. You may seek to be empowered or to understand something better.

The next step is crafting your intention. Be specific about it. Some people make the mistake of setting general intentions like, "I'd like to know about my financial life." However, it would be more effective to say, "I seek guidance in my present financial situation to understand my strengths and weaknesses and find the opportunities to elevate my finances." When you get very specific with your intention, it makes the reading more focused.

A crucial part of setting intentions is to ensure that you remain receptive. You need to be open to whatever messages you receive. Sometimes, readers will receive messages that they don't agree with, but that doesn't mean the messages aren't true. The last thing you want to do is doubt the cards. When you habitually do this, you're essentially shutting down your intuition and creating a state where your readings are always riddled with uncertainty and, therefore, never accurate. You must stay open and avoid letting your preconceived notions cloud what the card shares with you.

Cleansing and Charging the Deck

Now you have a sacred space and a clear intention. The next step is to cleanse and charge your deck. You cannot skip this step because it is important to eliminate stale, negative energies accumulated on the card and imbue the cards with positive energy that will be good for the reading. You can use the following methods to cleanse your deck.

1. Smudging is a powerful, popular method for cleansing places, people, and things. To "smudge" means to pass the thing you want to cleanse through some smoke. The smoke is often from cleansing herbs like Palo Santo, white sage, or cedar. You will need an incense burner so that you do not hurt yourself. When you light the herbs,

you can pass the deck through the smoke. As you do this, envision the smoke removing all negative energies attached to the cards.

2. Another method for cleansing the deck is using salt. Salt cleansing is putting your deck into a container with a little salt and letting it sit overnight. Esoterically, salt is an excellent substance for getting rid of negative or still energies. The next day, brush off all the salt from your cards.

3. You can also give your cards a moonlight bath. This is a great way for you to not only cleanse but charge your deck. All you have to do is set it under the full moon's light. Ensure that it is safe where the elements will not get to your cards and ruin them. You should let them sit in the moonlight overnight so that they can absorb the energies from the moon.

4. Finally, you can try visualization. All you have to do is hold the cards in both hands and then, in your mind, imagine a bright golden light emanating from your hands, surrounding the cards, burning away all negative and stale energies, and charging the cards.

Now that your cards have been cleansed, here are some charging techniques.

1. You can charge your cards with sunlight. It's the same as with moonlight. All you have to do is set your deck of cards somewhere the Sun's light can touch it for hours. It would be best if you worked with the early morning or late afternoon Sun, as the last thing you want is for the Sun to cause the pictures and colors on your card to fade. In your mind, assume the Sun sends energy that charges your cards with love and positivity.

2. You may also work with crystals. All crystals have energy. You can use these energies to charge the deck. You can figure out which crystal you want to charge your deck with some research. For instance, if you want to specialize in love and romance, you can work with the rose quartz crystal. If you are unsure which crystal to choose for your readings, you may work with clear quartz, which acts as an energy amplifier and goes well with every intention. You may also use amethyst because that stone is known to enhance psychic and intuitive abilities necessary for cartomancy. All you have to do is set the stone on top of your deck for hours or leave it overnight. The cards will take on the positive energy of the crystals. You must make a habit of charging and cleansing your crystals, too.

3. Yet another method to charge your deck involves intentional breathing. All you have to do is hold the deck up to your face and breathe in. As you exhale, imagine that that breath has your intention, and positive energy flows from it and into the cards.
4. You could also work with affirmations. All you have to do is hold the cards in your hands and state positive affirmations like, "I now charge you with love, wisdom, and truth."

Choosing a Spread or Layout

Another important part of preparing for your reading is figuring out the spread or layout you want to work with. To do this, you must think about the purpose of your reading. If you want guidance and something specific or are looking for broad strokes, you will find that those things will affect the spread you choose.

Next, you must consider the complexity and size of your spread. For instance, if you're looking for a simple, generalized answer, you may opt for a one-card draw. However, if you want something more nuanced in detail, you may choose something with multiple cards. If you don't have a lot of time, you may want a spread that doesn't have too many cards involved. If you've got time and you're looking for much deeper insight, it would be best to go with the largest possible layouts.

Formulating Questions

To ask clear questions, take time to reflect on what it is you're going through right now. What is it about? Gather all your feelings and thoughts about the circumstance first. Next, consider the main issue with the circumstance for which you need clarity. When you're clear about what the main objective of your reading is, it's time to craft your question. Make sure that they are specific. It does not help to ask broad questions like "What could the future hold?" Instead, you need to be very specific. For instance, ask, "What can I do to ensure that my relationship continues to improve?"

Note that you will get specific guidance when you are specific with your question. So don't be afraid to get very precise. If time is important regarding the situation, you must incorporate that element into your question. For instance, ask whether you should attend a seemingly important event at a certain time. It is important to specify when the time is, too. Is it within the next two months or in 3 years? Work that into your question.

Go with open-ended questions. These questions will allow the cards to answer you with lots of insight. Asking simple yes or no questions isn't the way to go in cartomancy. You want to ask questions that will cause you to reflect deeply.

Once you finally have your question, reflecting on it and refining it is important. Consider whether it captures everything you seek to understand about your situation and whether it agrees with your intentions for the reading. If you discover you must make adjustments, then do so. When you finally have it clear in your mind, write the question down so that your intention for the reading is fixed in your mind.

Developing Personal Interpretations

Getting better at cartomancy means practicing working with your intuition and fine-tuning that skill. Here are some things you can do to interpret the cards like a pro. First, you should study the cards and get familiar with them. After all, you cannot try to explain what you haven't taken the time to understand. So, think about the imagery, the colors, the various archetypes connected to the card, and so on. This book has provided ample information about the cards you could begin with.

Next, it is important that you just trust your intuition. Whenever a voice speaks up, trust it. It could be an actual voice or just a sense of knowing. It could be a thought with a distinctly different quality than your usual mental chatter. When you feel energy, don't question it or second guess it. Accept that this energy is the truth. With time, you'll discover that you are a lot more confident and your intuition.

Journaling is a good practice to have after each reading. You should write down everything you understood from the reading, the impressions you got from each card, and so on. These notes that you're making should always be reviewed. When you do this, you strengthen your ability to understand each card and interpret them accurately, depending on the context.

Another useful thing to help you with personal interpretations of these cards is to use active imagination exercises so that you can connect with them deeply. The visualization meditation you were offered is a great tool for this.

Consider your personal connection and meanings when it comes to the various images, colors, and symbols on the card. For instance, a card may remind you of a person or event. Do not discount your personal meanings just because they do not align with the traditional interpretations of the card. There may be a way to marry those meanings so that you can understand exactly what is being communicated to you by the divine.

Consider working with other cartomancers in your field. Because when you share your experiences with them, and they share theirs with you, you may pick up a thing or two. It is always a good idea to be open to new ways of doing things. Therefore, connecting with others is good, and staying open and curious will do wonders for your practice. A final note is that you must work with the cards regularly. You can't expect to work with them occasionally and somehow develop proficiency. Do a daily practice, and you will see phenomenal results over time.

Now that you know what you must do to perform a reading, it's time to look at some sample readings to try your hand at the real thing. Head on to the next chapter for this.

Chapter 7: Sample Readings

Sample readings are essential because they help you practice and use your skills appropriately. This chapter's main goal is to offer practical examples of how cartomancy can be applied in real life.

Sample Three-Card Spread Reading

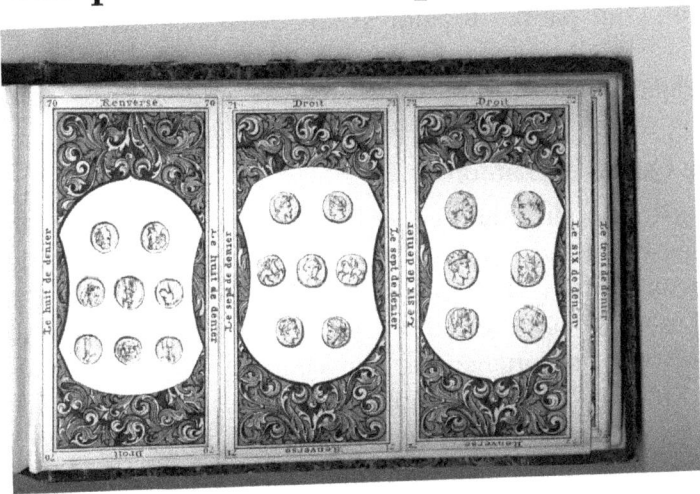

Sample three-card spread.[12]

Question: I suspect my partner is cheating on me as she claims to be faithful but posts certain things on social media that would imply to others that she's not in a relationship. Do I have anything to worry about regarding our relationship?

Cards drawn: Ace of Hearts, 5 of Spades, Queen of Diamonds

Card 1: Ace of Hearts

This card represents a new start. It's all about finally feeling fulfilled emotionally and finding the love you have long sought. In the context of the question, this card implies that your relationship is set on a firm foundation rooted in love and true connection. The connection between you and your partner is genuine, and you both feel deep affection for one another. It states that the bond cannot easily be broken and that if you both allow it, there is a potential for you to create something beautiful that lasts a lifetime. Look at everything going on with your relationship and cherish it. It's asking you to do what you can to foster this relationship so that it continues to improve.

Cards 2: 5 of Spades

This card represents conflict, obstacles, and challenges. It suggests you and your partner may butt heads now and then, experiencing difficult situations and having disagreements. However, you must not be quick to make assumptions or jump to conclusions. The 5 of Spades tells you that forces outside your relationship or misunderstandings could create tension. You may be misinterpreting this tension as possible infidelity. Therefore, you must do your best to stay open. Communicate your feelings with your partner to address any issues that may crop up in that conversation. By choosing to communicate, you create a situation where your challenges can easily be overcome, and not only that, your relationship can be stronger and better for it.

Card 3: Queen of Diamonds

This card embodies the energies of loyalty, stability, and practicality. Considering your question, this card tells you your partner is the bastion of stability and loyalty. The Queen of Diamonds stays faithful no matter what and always has the bigger picture in her mind. This person understands the importance of her connections and intends to stay committed to you. This card implies that your partner wants nothing but to ensure you both have a strong, long-lasting foundation. Therefore, this card asks you to trust that your partner is truly faithful to you and appreciate that.

Sample Celtic Cross Reading

Question: My sister and her husband threw me out of their home when I was in a vulnerable position with my mental health, and they never reached out to me once in 8 years. Finally, they have and claim they want to make amends and help me financially. Still, I suspect they're only planning to use me in a scheme against a step-sibling I'm close to (the person they've taken to court over frivolous claims). How should I approach their offer to help?

Card 1 — The Present: 3 of Hearts

This card suggests healing and a chance to reconcile with your family. It implies that the situation may offer a chance to fix the hurts from the past and mend broken bridges. It tells you that you have a shot here to forgive and be forgiven and understand each other.

Card 2 — Current Challenge: 10 of Diamonds

In this context, the ten of diamonds implies that what you are facing right now is whether or not your sister and her husband's offer to assist you is sincere. This card asks you to be careful in considering their intentions for you.

Card 3 — Distant Past: King of Clubs

The energy of the King of Clubs is someone who has authority and a strong will. In the past, there were power dynamics that did not favor you in your relationship with your family. The constant conflict led to misunderstandings. Perhaps you were labeled the black sheep. This card asks you to consider the dynamics between yourself and this person (your sister and her husband in this situation). Think about how their actions have affected your current situation and how likely it is that they may have changed.

Card 4 — Recent Past: 8 of spades

The 8 of Spades is a card that represents challenges on your path. Not too long ago, you had to deal with limitations and difficulties that stressed you mentally. These situations may have been further aggravated by the fact that you were thrown out of your home. Therefore, this card indicates that you were struggling terribly at that time and probably still are.

Card 5 — Best Outcome: Queen of Hearts

This card represents the energy of nurturing and compassion. It is all about being supported emotionally. If you accept your sister and her husband's proposal, do so cautiously while keeping your heart open, as there is a chance that you can be truly reconciled to each other.

Card 6 — Future Influence: 7 of Diamonds

The 7 of Diamonds tells you that there is a chance for you to grow financially. So, when it comes to the assistance being offered, there is a possibility that your financial situation could be better. However, it would be wise for you to be discerning. In other words, if you accept their help, it is important not to put yourself in a position where you will remain indebted to them. In fact, it may be best to tell them that you accept their offer and are thankful for it, but that does not automatically mean that they gain access to you or the right to control you as they did in the past.

Card 7 — Inner Emotions: Ace of Spades

This card represents new beginnings and fresh changes. Regarding your internal emotions, the card clarifies that you are very skeptical about their intentions. You really want to believe they have only the best intentions for you, but you can't help but be uncertain. You want a fresh start with them, but you are clearly troubled that this may be more of the same old dynamics you've already experienced with them. You need to trust your instincts and listen to your intuition to discern if or when you must remove yourself from interactions where they are concerned.

Card 8 — External Influences: 2 of Spades

This card represents challenges and obstacles. So, in this case, the challenge is the court case that involves your step-sibling. There is a great possibility that your sister and her husband are reaching out to you only because they feel like you would be a critical part of them winning the case they have with your step-sibling. It is up to you to decide if you want to accept their help while being clear if the time comes that you are not willing to be blackmailed into doing the wrong thing.

Card 9 — Hopes and Fears: Jack of Diamonds

This card is about being practical and resourceful in your ways. It demonstrates that you have hope that this could be the thing that finally plants you solidly on your feet financially. However, you are afraid that you will only be taken advantage of or become entangled in something that betrays your step-sibling.

Card 10 — Final Outcome: 4 of Clubs

This card tells you that your choices must be structured and ordered. In other words, you must be practical about this situation. There is a chance that you could finally be uplifted financially, as it sounds like you have been struggling with that. Just because you were suspicious of their intentions does not mean you should completely shove them aside, as they may be willing to offer you the help you need. You must, however, remain in touch with your instincts so that if it becomes obvious that they are attempting to weasel their way back into your life to control you, you can promptly cut ties. In the meantime, ask questions, and be honest with them and yourself.

Sample Three-Card Spread Reading

Question: Lately, I've felt the need to get more serious with my spiritual life. Still, I don't know where to start - how can I develop a bond with my higher self?

Card 1 – The Past: Queen of Hearts

Since this card represents compassion, you may have had certain experiences that piqued your spiritual curiosity and made you aware that there's much more to life than meets the eye. These experiences served as the seed for your present desire to connect with your spiritual nature. In your past, you experienced things that triggered you to become deeply sensitive to the subtle energies of the spiritual realm. In other words, you already have a good foundation to begin your spiritual exploration.

Card 2 – The Present: 8 of Diamonds

This card represents your discipline and practicality in manifesting the abundance that awaits you. The card implies that to connect with your higher self, finding disciplined and practical methods to help you along your path would be best. In other words, whatever spiritual path you choose should be structured and grounded. This is because these are the paths most likely to be effective at demonstrating to you just how spiritual you are. Therefore, you should study spiritual teachings with verifiable, observable impacts and results.

Card 3 – The Future: Ace of Spades

The Ace of Spades is the card of new spiritual insights and changes. This card tells you that you will experience a profound connection with your higher self in the future. This means that you will spiritually awaken and transform. The wisdom and insight you will receive as you walk your spiritual path will be life-changing. The Ace of Spades also implies that you will experience many opportunities to develop and grow as a spiritual being and connect with your higher self even more strongly than you can imagine.

Question: Lately, I've noticed that my body isn't acting like it used to. I am concerned but don't want to trouble myself needlessly. What must I be aware of to ensure I remain physically whole and youthful?

(Please note that you should always seek medical attention from a licensed professional if you feel there's something wrong with your body. Cartomancy is only a tool to give you further insight, not to diagnose you.)

Card 1 – The Present: Joker

The Joker is a card of unpredictability. It implies being flexible and having a sense of humor. Now, in the context of the question asked, the Joker represents the current situation that your body is going through. There are changes in its usual function that have you concerned. The Joker asks you to consider these changes with a flexible and open mindset. You are being asked to embrace the change and find a balance between caring for yourself and letting yourself enjoy life. The Joker tells you that not everything should be taken seriously and that it would be best to maintain a sense of humor about your health, as this will do wonders for it in the long run.

Card 2 – The Challenge: Queen of Hearts

The Queen of Hearts represents your emotional well-being. This card is about your intuition and your ability to nurture yourself. Related to your question, the card tells you that the challenge is trying to understand your emotions, which may have a powerful impact on your physical health. What you think is a physical problem is actually rooted in your emotions. The card tells you that you must pay attention to your feelings and do what you can to bring yourself more joy, laughter, and fulfillment. It is a good idea to ensure you have supportive relationships full of love and positivity. When you take care of your emotional well-being, it reflects on your body positively.

Card 3 – Guidance and Outcome: 7 of Diamonds

This card represents the ideas of being resourceful and practical. It is also about financial matters. Relative to your question, the card implies that it would be best to notice what you need physically. For instance, your body may ask you for more rest, exercise, or better nutrition. Therefore, you need to be practical in solving your current physical challenges. This card tells you that you should also consider investing money into maintaining your health and making decisions that will ultimately benefit you.

In summary, this reading asks you to be at peace with the changes that your body experiences, invest in taking care of yourself, and take the time to make sure you feel good emotionally. Put money into yourself and your health because you deserve it. Try to find balance in every part of your life, and you will find that your concerns are not much to worry about.

Now that you've seen a few readings, it is time for you to take your craft to the next level by working with your intuition. You're going to discover how in the next chapter. But first, let's talk about intuition. What is it?

Chapter 8: Intuitive Readings

What Is Intuition?

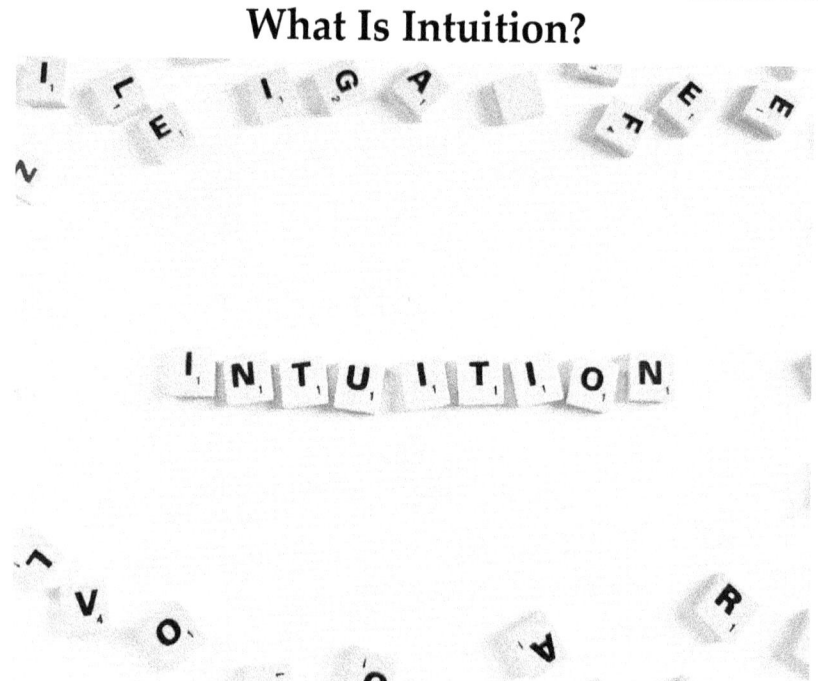

Intuition is a force beyond logic and reason.[18]

Intuition has been mentioned several times in this book. But the question is, what is it, truly? Intuition is something that exists in everyone. You can think of it as an ancient mystical force responsible for the evolution of consciousness as it is today. Intuition is something that is beyond the bounds of logic and reason. It comes from your soul, that voice that tells you things that are spot on. Intuition is when you get sudden knowledge about something in a way that you cannot quite describe. You just know it's true, and when you check on your hunch, you discover you were right about it. Your intuition is that aspect of you that uncovers all the secrets of the universe and lets you know what's happening beneath the surface of every situation.

It is important to realize that intuition is not just a fleeting thought. It is not something that you deduce by logical thinking. It is much more than that. Most logically-inclined people tend to assume that intuition is the same thing as a deduction, but it is not. Intuition involves emotions and a deep inner knowing that comes from beyond your mind. It ripples through the essence of your soul and being. Intuition can communicate to you through various means, such as synchronicity, signs, and symbols all around you.

Interestingly, intuition also surpasses the bounds of time and space. It doesn't matter whether you're dealing with your past, present, or future. Intuition can make itself available, revealing everything you need to know about any time in your life or any experience you might have had.

When performing cartomancy, you must be in touch with this inner wisdom you carry. Unfortunately, many people have dulled this sense because they continue to indulge in habits that do not serve their intuition. For instance, if you spend a lot of time on social media or indulge in certain substances that affect or alter your consciousness, you may find your intuitive edge dull. However, there's nothing to worry about because you can always sharpen it when you want to. And you will learn just how to do that to have the most intuitive, bang-on readings during your cartomancy sessions.

How Intuition Works

Attuning yourself to sense subtle energies: To conduct intuitive readings, it is important for you to first understand the mechanics of intuition. The first thing involves sensing what is unseen or undetectable to your five senses. When you can connect to the unseen, you've opened yourself up to the secrets in the spiritual realm. If you don't already know this, know that everything physical is rooted in the spiritual world. In other words, the spiritual energy permeates everything and everyone that exists. Consequently, by developing your intuition, you set up a situation where you are more open to picking up the subtle energies of spirit, which implies that you can access any information you want regardless of space or time. This is because the spiritual aspect of life transcends those two boundaries of space and time.

Paying attention to your inner wisdom: The next step in connecting to your intuition involves listening to your inner wisdom. Once you can attune yourself to subtle energies by using practices like meditation, you must teach yourself to listen to the inner voice that speaks within you. Everyone has this voice, but the more you practice paying attention to it, and the better you are at picking up subtle energies, the louder is voice will be. It'll be tough to mistake it for anything else.

Some people assume that these voices are a result of mental conditions like schizophrenia, or they feel that these voices are pretty much the same as a thought that you have in your head, but that's not the case at all. Something about intuition speaking usually freezes you in your tracks and causes you to take stock of the present moment as all time and space lose meaning. You know deep within yourself that the information you're getting is accurate. Listening to the wisdom within you means you must tune out the world's noise outside and focus all your attention on the inside.

Trusting strange things: The next thing you must do after tuning yourself to subtle energies and learning to listen to your inner voice is to trust what feels unfamiliar. This is important because intuitive messages will often show up in ways that are not the norm for you. After all, how else are they supposed to get your attention? Intuition can be a gut feeling, knowing, a hunch that you're right about something, or even a flash of insight. To get better at working with your intuition and having it be more accurate, you must learn to trust it in whatever form it shows up for you. Do not fall into the trap of questioning whether or not what it shares with you is true. Intuition is one of those things where *when you know, you know*.

Paying attention to symbols and synchronicity: Recognizing synchronicity and symbolism is a huge part of understanding your intuition and working with it. Symbols are the language of the subconscious. Synchronicity is how your soul attempts to communicate with you through your intuition. Synchronicity is the unlikeliness of certain events happening simultaneously or in line with one another in a way that cannot be logically explained. It involves seeing a certain number pattern repeating itself or having a set of events play out so beautifully that you could not have imagined it. You need to learn to recognize synchronicity and other symbols that can pop up in your daily life. The more attention you pay to these things and listen to your intuition, the more you can learn about life.

Working on being in the present: Developing mindfulness is the next thing you must consider. In other words, you must teach yourself to be in the here and now. Often, most people are stuck ruminating about their past or worrying about their future but never really pay attention to what's happening here and now. For you to connect with your intuition, you must be present. This is because intuition thrives in the here and now. So, if you're hoping to get guidance from this inner wisdom you carry daily, you must master the art of always staying grounded in the present. And the way to do this is by practicing being mindful. Meditation is one way you can achieve mindfulness.

Accepting the wisdom of your heart: It is funny that many assume that wisdom only comes from the brain. However, this is not always the case. Your heart has a wisdom of its own. That wisdom is intuition. You must learn the language of emotions because this is how your intuition will often speak to you. That's not to say that intuition is only about how you feel. However, you need to know what your heart tells you at every point in time because that is how you get better at working with your intuition. Your intuition is not a logical thing. It is mostly emotional. Therefore, by getting familiar with your emotional landscape, you will find yourself accessing amazing wells of knowledge you could never have fathomed.

With all this said, the question is, how do you perform an intuitive reading? How can you develop and harness your intuition in the practice of cartomancy?

Well, you're about to discover just how!

You already know two excellent methods to get in touch with your intuition and develop it. As discussed in the previous chapter, you can use meditation and visualization exercises. However, the following are ways you can develop your intuition to have more intuitive readings.

Mindful Observation

Mindful observation is exactly the way it sounds. It is all about paying attention to everything happening within and around you. It is about noticing your environment, thoughts, feelings, emotions, and sensations.

The more you pay attention to these things, the more present you will feel, which is a bonus for your intuitive readings. Here's how to practice mindful observation:

1. First, you must find somewhere quiet where you will not be distracted or disturbed for at least 10 to 15 minutes. Ensure that this location allows you to relax easily and wear comfortable clothing.

2. Sit in a position that is comfortable for you. If you like, you can sit cross-legged, or you can sit on a chair. Put your hands on your thighs or just rest them in your lap however you want to.

3. Take some time to ground yourself. This means you will shut your eyes and take a few deep breaths in through your nose and out through your mouth. Allow your body to get less tense with each exhale. Notice the weight of your body and allow it to let go of all the tension you feel.

4. Notice your breath. This is basically the same as meditation. Sit with your breath and observe it as it goes in and out.

5. Now, it's time to go beyond this by expanding your awareness. This implies that you will begin to allow other information besides your breath to filter into your mind. Start noticing your thoughts, how you feel, and the emotions you are sensing. Notice them as they come up but do your best not to judge any of them. Don't get attached, as you're just observing.

6. It's time to bring your senses into the game. Notice the smells, sights, and sensations you're picking up with your five senses. You must engage with every sensory impression as fully as you can.

7. Do your best to remain non-judgmental. Continue to observe all these things and let go of the need to attach a label to any of them. Just observe curiously and with acceptance.

8. When your mind inevitably wanders from the exercise, as it will, just gently bring it back to the present. Get back to focusing on your breath and your observations. It is all about being aware, so keep that in mind.

9. Finally, you must practice this as often as you can. This is how you get better at being mindfully observant.

Now, you're probably wondering the difference between this exercise and the meditation exercise you were given before. Remember that where the meditation exercise has you only focusing on your breath, this mindful observation exercise is about you becoming aware of other things besides your breath that will help you be rooted in the present moment.

Intuitive Exercises

Intuitive exercises are wonderful tools for helping you get better at using your intuition during cartomancy. Here's how you can get involved with them.

1. Pick an exercise. For instance, you may choose an exercise like trying to guess what's in a sealed envelope or intuitively picking cards from a deck, guessing what's on the card, before flipping it around to see if you were correct.
2. Now that you know the exercise you want, set your intention. Your intention involves getting better at working with your intuition and getting accurate information. You can state the sensation out loud or in your mind.
3. Make sure you're somewhere where the weather is no disturbance or distraction. If it helps, you can set up the ambiance with perfect lighting, music, and even incense.
4. It's time to relax and calm yourself with a few breaths. When you feel like your mind is clear and your body is relaxed, you can move on to the next step.
5. Begin guessing what's in your sealed envelopes. Let your intuition be your guide, and don't try to rush the process. It is important to note that there is no force in the process regarding your intuition. So be as relaxed and at ease as you can be. If you notice that you're picking the wrong things or making the wrong guesses, it is important not to be hard on yourself because that may only cause you to have even worse results.
6. When you've finished your exercise, reflect on your results. Compare how accurate your guesses were this time as opposed to the last time. And also, it is important to ensure that you practice regularly.

Other Tools to Sharpen Intuition

In addition to the tools offered so far, there are other things you can do to sharpen your intuitive senses. Here is a quick look at them:

1. **Keep a journal.** When you keep a journal, you start to take stock of your life. It means that you become more aware of how you are changing and how your world is changing. Becoming aware naturally means you will become more sensitive to your intuitive voice. Consider writing down your dreams and every intuitive hunch you get. Also, when you notice something synchronistic going on, write it down. For instance, if you notice that you keep seeing a certain number all the time, it might be worth noting what's happening around you and the thoughts and feelings you were having when the number showed up. You may notice that there is a pattern there. Always review your journal. It's not just about writing things down but reading them later to help you start spotting intuition at work in your life.

2. **Try energy work.** You naturally become more sensitive to subtle energies when you do energy work such as Reiki or Qigong. As you already know, intuition can speak to you through subtle energies in addition to your emotions. Therefore, any form of energy work at all but help you to begin picking up on vibes. This goes even beyond cartomancy as you adapt to reading people because you've been practicing how to work with energy.

3. **Express yourself creatively.** Something about the creative process does wonders when opening up your intuitive abilities and making them more pronounced. You should do it, whether writing, painting, or making music. The wonderful thing about creative activities is that they're an excellent way for you to bypass your logical, rational mind and gain access to the intuitive side of yourself.

4. **It is a good idea to spend as much time around nature as you can.** The more time you spend in nature, connecting with a natural world that is naturally in alignment with spiritual energies and subtle energies, the better you will understand when it is your intuition speaking.

5. **Finally, you will find much value in solitude.** This doesn't mean you should never have friends, go out, or communicate with your family. It just means that you must practice finding time to retreat and be on your own each day. This is because you need to distinguish between your intuitive voice and your thoughts, as well as your intuitive voice versus those of other people around you. You need to be separated for a bit every day because that is how you become familiar with the

voice of spirit, and this will go a long way and help you with the accuracy of your readings.

Cultivating an Open Mind

Working with your intuition implies having an open and receptive mind. If your mind is closed off and constantly questioning things, then the odds are you will not have much success with your readings. Therefore, there are a few things that you should consider incorporating into your daily practices:

- Make a practice of clearing your mind before you start reading.
- Let go of the desire for a reading to go in a specific way. Every reading is unique and doesn't always have to play out how you think it should.
- Do your best not to judge. Your only job is to channel the message from the cards and nothing more. Playing judge, jury, and executioner during reading is not your job.
- You must develop trust for your inner wisdom. This is the only way you can continue to encourage your intuition to feed you all the information you need and pick up on it accurately.
- You must always be compassionate to yourself. You're just learning, which means you'll make some mistakes. It's not a good idea to beat yourself up just because you get some things wrong while learning to become a cartomancy master. So, give yourself some time and love.
- Take care of yourself physically, mentally, and emotionally, and you will discover that your intuition improves.

Follow all of the tips offered in this chapter. You will discover that you become better each day at working with your intuition in every situation, not just during your cartomancy readings. Now that you understand how to develop the muscle of your intuition, the question is: *is there more to cartomancy?* In the next chapter, you're going to learn some advanced cartomancy.

Chapter 9: Advanced Cartomancy

Hold on to your horses because the techniques you will learn in this chapter are not for the newbies. You could attempt them if you are new to cartomancy. Still, it would be much better for you to understand the basics before attempting either method.

The Wheel of Fortune Spread

In Tarot, there is a card known as the Wheel of Fortune. This card represents the energy of cycles, chance, changes, and fortune. Its darker aspects include repetition, destiny, fate, and recurrences. There is a spread that is based on this particular card. This spread is founded on the idea of seasons, reminiscent of the idea of cycles represented by the Wheel of Fortune. The thing about cycles is that you cannot escape them. And in the same way, you cannot turn back the hands of time.

As you pay attention to life's seasons, you realize there is a time to act and another to hang back and observe. It is important to detect the harmonies that are naturally inherent in life so that we can flow with them. Most people live their

Wheel of Fortune tarot card represents change.[14]

lives trying to force things to happen when they should be resting or hibernating. Humans are not divorced from nature. Therefore, you must follow its rhythm. Otherwise, you will find yourself living a life of misery. This is the wisdom embodied in the Wheel of Fortune card and the concept of the wheel itself.

A good time to use this spread is when you want to look at your life's events from a broad perspective or see how your year has been so far and how your life has changed since the start of a new year.

The Wheel of Fortune spread has six cards. The first card to be dealt is the Self card in the middle and to the left. It represents what your current state is. The second card is the Environment card, which goes to the right of the Self card. This talks about the world you find yourself in and how it influences you and your actions. The third card is the Winter card, the solo card on top of the middle row of four. This card lets you know that it is time to rest or hibernate so that you can regain your strength. It talks about what you need to take a break from at the moment or what you need to renew.

The fourth card is the Spring card, which sits to the extreme left on the fourth row. This card tells you about your growth. It'll show you what is just coming to be in your life or what is building momentum.

The fifth, or summer card, is at the bottom of the entire spread and represents abundance. This is a time in your life when everything blooms fully. So, it calls you to appreciate or be thankful for the good in your life right now.

The sixth card is the fall card, the extreme right on the four-card row. This card represents losing or passing on. It's about what to let go of or what is leaving your life now.

Working with the Wheel of Fortune spread is easy now that you understand how these cards are laid out and their meanings. Remember that all you have to do is apply the concepts from previous chapters about interpreting cards relative to one another.

The Zodiac Tarot Spread

The Zodiac spread is also called the 12-house astrology spread. It is commonly used with a Tarot deck. You can read it in one or two ways, either informatively or predictively. In other words, you can read it by gleaning meaning from the astrological house of each card, or you can use each card to represent a month of the year and predict what your month may be like.

Since the Zodiac spread works with all the astrological houses, of which there are 12, it's a good spread for you to use when you're just looking for a general idea of where your life is going. The 12 astrological houses also represent the 12 different aspects of your life. So, if you want to ask some really pointed questions like what your love life will look like over the next year, this is an excellent spread to work with.

You need to know some things before you begin working with the spread. First, there are many variations of the Zodiac tarot spread, and you'll learn one of the easiest. If you have some knowledge of astrology, it might be worth looking into the other more complicated ways of working with this spread.

Another thing you must remember about the spread is that it's best to do it occasionally. In other words, this is not something that you work with every day to plan your weeks. It would be best to use this to plan out your year, or at least plan for each quarter. It's also an excellent spread to work with when it's your birthday. If you're worried about how you're supposed to remember all 12 of the astrological houses, the good thing is you can always find this information on the internet. You will work with 12 or 13 cards to set up the Zodiac tarot spread. The final decision is up to you. These cards are going to be set up in a circle.

First, shuffle and cut the deck, and then you put the first card at the far left. This card will be in the 9 o'clock position. Next, you will set the remaining cards on the table or counterclockwise, setting one card for every hour of your imaginary clock. If you're working with a 13th card, put that card in the middle of the circle you have created. It is important to know astrology because you must understand that each card represents the various houses and signs of the Zodiac, beginning with Aries.

The first card represents the **Sun sign**. Your Sun sign is the general astrological sign people ask you about when they ask what your sign is. The Sun sign is associated with the First House or the House of Self. It represents your general personality, how you view life and present yourself to the world. It's about how you see yourself and how others perceive you. This House also represents your health.

The second card represents the **House of Value and Possessions**. It demonstrates how you relate to your finances and your material possessions. It's about your sense of security in life and how much you can earn. The second card is about your self-worth too. It shows you the things that you value the most in life.

The third card represents the **House of Communication**. It's all about your family and the other people around you. It's about who knows you and who you know. But it's important to note that it does not include your children, spouse, or parents. This third card is about your travel as well. If you're working with a tarot, getting six swords in this placement may show that you just might be about to move to someplace new. Communication and writing are also under the purview of this third card.

The fourth card represents the fourth House, the **House of Home and Family**. It demonstrates your relationships with the people at home, especially with your children and parents. This card is a representation of all the attachments that you have gathered throughout your life. It's about your true roots and what domestic living is like for you. It's also the about your emotional stability and security, especially regarding familial ties.

The fifth card correlates with the fifth **House of Astrology**, the **House of Creativity**. It's about the things that you are most passionate about and how you express your emotions physically. This card is all about the hobbies you would like to do for fun and how you approach problem-solving. It's also quite informative about the kind of lover that you are to your significant other. With this card correlated to the 5th House, you can learn what you love in others and what makes you fall in love.

The sixth card is about your work and is associated with the **House of Service**. Not only does it demonstrate how healthy you are on the inside, but it also talks about your self-care, personal hygiene, the way you feed yourself, and so on. This card is about what your everyday habits are.

The seventh card represents your partnerships and correlates to the seventh **House of Relationships.** It is about how you treat the partnerships you have in your life, romantically or otherwise. It lets you know the kind of person who would work best with you regardless of your endeavor. Even enemies are partners, so keep that in mind as you read this card.

The eighth card represents your secrets. It's connected to the **House of Transformation**, all about everything nobody wants to discuss, like sex and death. Maybe even taxes. This card is about what others give you, like gifts, inheritances, or winning a prize or the lottery. Consider what this card holds for you whenever you want to make a big financial decision. The eighth House is the container of your life force and sexual power. In this context, sexual power is not about making love, which is the purview of the fifth House, but is more about the main driving force in your life.

The ninth card is connected to the **House of Purpose**, which is all about your personal growth and dreams. It's about how you can continue to stretch and expand your awareness. This includes travel, further education, philosophy, spirituality, and religion.

The tenth card represents your career and the **House of Social Status**. It represents how you appear. It's not about how you deliberately present yourself, as that would be the first House, but how others see you. It's about the way you are going about making your dreams happen and fulfilling the expectations that you have of yourself. This card has to do with your career and your financial position.

The eleventh card is connected to the **House of Friendships**. It is about your casual friendships, social connections, the people who know you, and how you interact with them. It's also all about charity, shedding light on how you feel about generosity, giving, and worthy causes.

The twelfth card represents your shadow self. It is correlated to the **12th House of Astrology, The House of the Subconscious**. Sometimes you may hear it ominously referred to as the **House of Sorrows**, and this is because it is deeply connected to the psychological issues that you have not addressed yet. This House demonstrates the things that weigh you down and keep you up at night and the self-imposed prison you have created around you through your limiting beliefs. It is a card that demonstrates the enemies that hide within that you may not be aware of, as well as dangers that you have not become conscious of yet. It is this card that will show you if you are living up to your life's potential or not.

Finally, there's the thirteenth card. This card demonstrates the overarching theme of the reading that you are conducting. It is an optional card; however, if you're working with it, it'll give you even more clarity on what the other cards are about.

Specialized Systems

There are specialized decks and systems that you can work with to make your cartomancy practice not only advanced but give you the most detailed interpretations and readings ever. You already know about some of these systems, like the Lenormand cards, Kipper cards, and Tarot cards. However, you can incorporate other specialized systems like rune stones, numerology, and astrology. These are just some ways to tweak your cartomancy readings for deeper meaning.

Runestones, for instance, are powerful ancient symbols in Norse divination. The stones are usually made of actual stones or wood. On each one, you'll find a runic symbol etched into it. Each symbol represents different aspects of life and offers guidance in its own way. To interpret runes accurately, you must understand what each means and determine what various combinations would imply. However, runes are outside the scope of this book. But if you were to learn about them, they would be a wonderful addition to your divination practice with cards.

You've already witnessed through the Zodiac spread how it's possible to incorporate astrology into your readings. However, knowing that you need not use only the Zodiac spread for astrological meanings is important. You can always incorporate astrology by assigning various astrological planets or meanings to the cards.

Numerology is also an excellent way to make your cartomancy system even more specialized. This has already been touched on in a previous chapter, where the significance of numbers was also discussed. It would be worthwhile to dive into numerology even further. Not only can you use numerology by working with the numbers already on the cards, but you can also work with the numbers by counting or taking note of the orders in which the cards were set down on the table during your reading.

When you mix and match different systems of cartomancy and divination, you will find that the results from your readings are powerful. This is because you have access to so many more symbols and meanings that it is impossible not to have a richer perspective of the situation you are asking questions about. You could combine different specialized decks or start off with a Tarot spread so you can understand general themes and then segue into a Lenormand deck to get the specifics. There are no hard and fast rules for practicing cartomancy.

The next chapter will explore the many different approaches to cartomancy. By looking at these different approaches, you will have a much more insightful understanding of how card reading works so that you can develop your own system.

Chapter 10: Different Approaches to Cartomancy

There are so many approaches you can take when it comes to cartomancy. There's no such thing as the one way that you should take. In fact, there are as many approaches as there are cartomancy practitioners. Therefore, you should not feel restricted to taking just one route. In this chapter, you'll learn about the different approaches you can work with to help you read the cards accurately and intuitively for yourself and the people who seek your services.

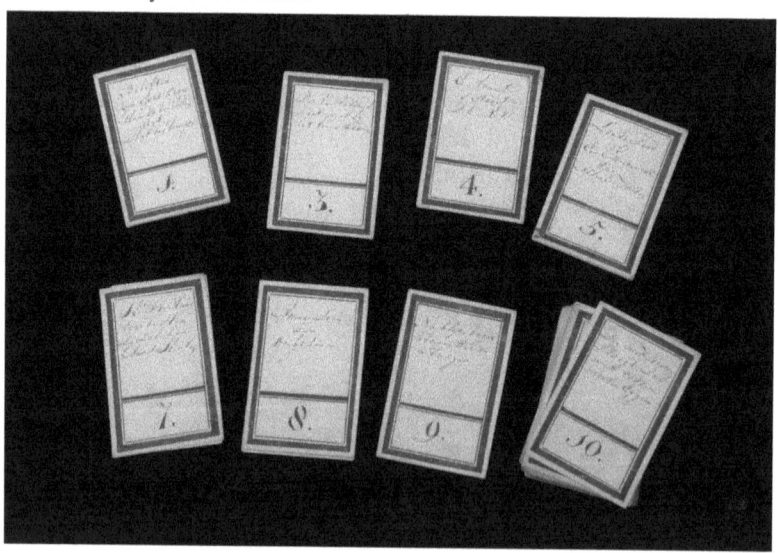

Many approaches can be taken to understand cartomancy.[15]

The Analytical Approach

When you're reading the cards using the analytical approach, it implies that you're taking really complex readings and breaking them down so that they're simpler and easier to understand. In other words, you're taking the whole and breaking it down into smaller parts, making it easier for you to use reason and logic to interpret what you're getting from the cards. You're doing some critical analysis and working systematically to discover the true meaning the cards are showing you.

The first thing is to analyze the cards one after the other. In other words, rather than figuring out how two cards generate an entirely new meaning outside of what each one represents, you should look at each card individually. You'll consider traditional meanings, what the card means to you personally, and its symbolism. Look at the colors and imagery on the card to figure out the impressions you're getting from it on an energetic level.

Working analytically means that you must also consider the relationships between the cards. So, think about how close they are in terms of positions (the closer the cards are in a spread, the stronger their influence on each other). Consider how they are in terms of orientation. Is there a card that is reversed next to one which is upright? Which card comes first? Think about the various connections, oppositions, or patterns they show up.

You must bring logic and reason into play. This means that you will use deductive reasoning and some critical thinking to determine what the card combinations are trying to tell you. This does not mean you won't use your intuition in this approach. However, you will rely mostly on your logical mind for this process.

You should have a set framework that allows you to easily analyze the cards every single time. You're definitely not going to get away with not paying attention to details when you choose the analytical method of cartomancy. This approach is about being as objective as possible when interpreting the cards.

Predictive Approach

Choosing the predictive route instead of the analytical route implies that you will interpret the cards to figure out what could happen in the future regarding a certain situation. You will also have to work with symbols here because you have to interpret the symbols' meanings relative to possible future results. Each card will have its unique archetype, energy, and situation that you can use to draw conclusions about what you could expect to come.

Another important element of this method of approach is the timing and progression of things. You may want to think about where the positions of the cards are, astrology, numerology, and other methodologies to figure out just when something happens, what will happen, and in what sequence. This makes it easier for you to create a timeline of possible events that may occur.

When working with a predictive approach, consider the probability of something specific happening over something else. In other words, you must consider that there will be alternatives to your possible future predictions. When you allow for some flexibility here, it gives you more room for nuanced predictions. It allows you to be better prepared for whatever scenario comes your way.

When working with a predictive approach, you must be as ethical as possible. In other words, if you're doing a reading for someone else, you must continue to let the querent understand that their results are not necessarily set in stone and can always change. You must support whoever asks questions by helping them understand that they are in charge of their destiny. There is no such thing as something being fixed in stone regarding their cartomancy results.

Therapeutic Approach

You can work with a therapeutic approach when you want to use the readings to help you grow personally or reflect on your life. You can also use this as a healing tool. The cards can help you understand what's going on with your health and well-being emotionally, psychologically, and spiritually. A therapeutic approach to cartomancy aims to help you become more aware of yourself – and can help with empowerment in that area.

This approach to reading the cards involves a lot of introspection and self-reflection. Because the cards act as a mirror that shows you how you've been thinking and feeling both consciously and subconsciously and how all of this has come together to create the life that you have lived so far, another thing to note is that you must explore your emotions when working with this approach. You should think about your emotions and what's causing them. In other words, the cards will act as a shovel to dig beneath the surface and uncover whatever is lying beneath emotionally. This way, you can let go of the blockages holding you back from experiencing clarity and progress in life.

The therapeutic approach also implies that you will use the cards to help you heal whatever wounds you suffer emotionally and spiritually. You can use the cards with this approach to deal with the challenges and obstacles on your path to feel more empowered and take control of your life.

This approach also implies working with symbols and metaphors. You must be in touch with your empathetic and compassionate side because it is important not to be judgmental while making inquiries on your or another person's behalf. With this method, you can set your intentions and goals based on the information you get from the cards. If you choose, you can also integrate this therapeutic approach of cartomancy with other therapies such as psychotherapy, counseling, or energy healing. All of this will augment the results you get from your card reading sessions.

The Narrative Approach

In cartomancy, the narrative approach involves working with stories to understand what the cards say. As a reader, crafting a narrative that offers insights and clear guidance is your job. One of the first things you must do is create the storyline, which means you must look at the cards as if they are trying to tell you a story. You must consider the cards as one, looking for the characters, plot lines, and other elements you typically find in a story.

Another important element of this narrative approach requires considering the sequence of the cards in their placements. This sequencing will offer you more understanding as you craft the story, which must come from intuition. You shouldn't feel like you're forcing the process. As you read the cards in a story format, you can call upon your personal experiences to help you flesh out their message. Besides your personal experience, you should incorporate universal archetypes and symbolism to deliver a reading that accurately captures the cards' messages.

The Experimental Approach

Cartomancy is a field that has continued to evolve over time. This implies that new methods and technologies are being crafted daily to take advantage of reading the cards' information. When you're working with the experimental approach, it means that you must keep an open and receptive mind, one that is willing to think outside of the box. It means that you must be willing to adapt to the times. These days, everything is digital. Therefore, you must be willing to accept that digital readings can be and indeed are valid.

The experimental approach to reading cards means you must work with technology to see how it can help you. This means creating digital tools and platforms your end user can easily access to get the necessary information they seek. The upside to working with technology is that you do not necessarily need to be present for your querent to get a reading. If the end user of your digital platform is in touch with their intuition and keeps an open mind, there is nothing to worry about. Their reading will be as accurate and useful as that from an in-person, traditional cartomancy session. Naturally, the energies of the spiritual world, which permeate everything, will also work through the programming and deliver the messaging required by the querent.

Being an experimentalist also implies that you should be at peace with creating new spreads to tackle unique situations. Sure, you have been offered a plethora of ways that you can work with cards. However, that does not mean you cannot create your own spreads. After all, the common spreads used today were created by someone, weren't they? So, as an experimental cartomancer, nothing stops you from doing your own thing if you find it more efficient. You must ensure that you're working with your intuition to create the right spread or make the right changes at the right time contextually. For instance, you may be intuitively led to combine several systems uniquely, giving you much deeper insight into far more comprehensive readings than usual.

Experimentalist cartomancy also implies working collaboratively. You may have to work with other readers and practitioners to interpret the cards. This could be beneficial because other readers may have certain pieces of the puzzle that you may have been missing from your own interpretations, or it may help you see things in a new light that you find beneficial to your own readings going forward.

Another interesting thing with the experimental approach to cartomancy is that you can work with artistic elements to help you better divine your card's messages. This could include designing new forms of cards that add interesting elements to a reading. You may even want to incorporate visuals and performative art, which is possible thanks to new technologies.

Being able to personalize your practice is a key tenet of experimental cartomancy. In other words, you should create certain routines, rituals, and methodologies that work for you in particular rather than go along with a general prescription for this craft. When you personalize practice like this, it enhances your results. You'll find that your readings are very accurate, and you seldom have to wonder what the cards say because you have a proven, working system.

Finally, there's the unmistakable aspect of constant research and exploration. This means combing through the old ways of doing things and looking at emerging technologies and methodologies to craft newer, better ways of receiving information from the spirit realm through the cards.

Figuring Out Your Approach

Suppose you're wondering what the best approach to take is regarding cartomancy. In that case, it will depend on your beliefs about the craft and your goals and preferences. For one thing, you must self-reflect. Think about the things that interest you and where your strengths lie. Think about whether you're more of an analytical thinker (which means the analytical approach is for you) or if you do better with your feeling (which could imply that you should be better as an intuitive cartomancer). Suppose you are inclined toward therapeutic work and love to tinker and experiment. That should tell you that you would do well with a blend of therapeutic and experimental approaches.

The next thing you must do is to get familiar with the various approaches. This means you will have to read several books, watch videos on YouTube, and do intense research to figure out the different philosophies surrounding cartomancy because there are many. You can even attend workshops and take courses to learn from experienced people to see what floats your boat. This exploration period will help you determine the different perspectives and develop your unique blend of approaches.

It is important to note that there will be an inevitable trial-and-error phase where you try to see what works and what doesn't. It will help if you continue practicing and noting what works for you. Notice how your experience goes and how connected you feel to the cards and the reading process. Pay attention to how much more accurate you are when using one methodology over another. You'll inevitably craft your unique method of working with the cards by constantly experimenting like this.

It would be remiss not to mention that your intuition will be a big factor here. So, you should always trust the guidance you get from within as you work to determine your approach. If you feel something is wrong for you, don't hesitate to drop it. If it works, it should be a part of your cartomancy arsenal.

Having someone to act as your mentor would be helpful. Work with those who are more experienced than you are. Seek out communities of those doing the same thing as you are, and you will find yourself getting better at what you do and gradually creating a niche for yourself. Now, what are you going to do with all this information? The ball is in your court. May Spirit guide you on your journey with the cards!

Conclusion

You've finally come to the end of this book, and at this point, you should know enough about cartomancy for you to begin your journey. Remember that this is something that requires your intuition to take the lead. This means you must approach the practice with trust and faith. Have a lot of curiosity and zero expectations about how it will play out for you.

Many beginners fall into the trap of feeling frustrated and angry with themselves because they are not getting the results that they had hoped for. You mustn't fall into this trap. This craft, like any other skill, will take time to learn. Therefore, be patient with yourself, and trust that the more you work with your intuition, just like any muscle, the stronger it will get.

Cartomancy is a powerful skill that you can use to better not just your life but the lives of those around you. It is a worthy endeavor to be a part of, and the fact that you have chosen this book and read it through to this point indicates that you must be called to practice this craft. Whenever you feel frustrated about your results, remember that it's not a matter of **_if_** you'll get better – but **_when_**.

There is no point in reading this book if you do not practice what you've learned! Just because you understand how something works does not mean you are automatically a professional. In the same way, you would not expect to be a professional driver just by reading a book about driving or watching a video. You have to put in the work yourself.

Therefore, you should get your first deck and get to know your cards as soon as possible. When things finally start to click, you'll wonder how you could ever have lived without consulting the cards!

Part 2: Celtic Symbolism

The Ultimate Guide to the Spiritual Meaning of Symbols of the Celts and Their Use in Paganism

Introduction

The ancient Celtic culture has been attracting the attention and curiosity of people for centuries due to its rich traditions, fascinating mythology, and deep connection to nature. The Celts were a diverse group of people inhabiting various parts of Europe, and they left behind a rich legacy of symbolism that holds profound meaning to this day. This book explores the deep and captivating realm of Celtic spirituality and symbolism and teaches a few things about the Celtic heritage and its significance. Apart from spirituality, the Celtic culture is a complicated tapestry woven with intricate threads of music, art, folklore, and mysticism.

Although the Celts are mainly considered Irish people, they were also inhabitants of Scotland and Wales. They are most well-known for their deep affinity for the natural world, their sacred reverence for the cycles of nature, and the spirits that reside within this world. The vibrant festivals and celebrations held by the Celtic people attract the most attention from outsiders, but the mysterious symbolism makes this culture great. Symbols have played a central role in Celtic spirituality and served as the primary way the Celts communicated with the divine. Each symbol has a spiritual significance and a deeper meaning behind it.

To understand and unravel the mysterious world of Celtic symbolism, one must first acknowledge the significance of the natural world in Celtic spirituality. Paganism and its ties to nature, the earth, the natural elements, and spirits form the cornerstone of Celtic spirituality. For instance, with its strength and long life, the mighty oak tree represents wisdom and endurance, while the flowing rivers and sacred springs symbolize life's natural cycles. The Celts believe that the beautiful interplay of these elements is essential to uncovering the deeper mysteries of this world.

The intricate knots and spirals in Celtic symbols, also known as Celtic knots, hold special meaning in terms of spirituality. The interwoven lines and circles are representative of the interconnectedness of all things and the eternal nature of life. Although aesthetically interesting, Celtic symbols are not simply decorative motifs but representative of deeper spiritual meanings with themes of unity, eternity, and divine mysteries. The Celts truly believed that studying these intricate patterns would help them unlock the deeper layers of this world.

Studying Celtic symbolism won't just give you a glimpse into the worldview of the ancient Celts and their rich cultural heritage, but it will also help you connect with their spiritual practices. However, as you approach this exploration, it's essential to be sensitive and have an open mind to the various beliefs discussed in this book. Whether you go through Celtic mythology or the meanings behind Celtic symbolism, you should approach the subject with a sense of curiosity instead of being judgmental or skeptical. While it's okay to be skeptical, it's unacceptable to mock a culture, religion, or its beliefs. So, open your mind and heart to the mysteries that lie ahead, and let the world of Celtic spirituality captivate you.

Chapter 1: The Ancient Celts

It is believed the ancient Celtic culture originates from different tribes who once inhabited the territories of Western and Central Europe from 700 B.C.E. to 400 C.E. Initially. These tribes shared a common language, culture, and religion. However, after migrating to various parts of the world and bringing along their rich heritage and culture, they began to create greater diversity among the Celts. The rise of the Roman Empire suppressed most of the Celtic culture from several territories. However, it still survived in remote parts of Europe, including Ireland and England, where it is still practiced. This chapter explores the culture, society, art, religion, warfare customs, burial practices, and other aspects of the lives of the ancient Celts.

People often relate the Celts to the United Kingdom (mostly Ireland and Scotland).[16]

Who Were the Ancient Celts?

Due to a lack of historical records, the exact origin of the Celts is still debated among historians. Over the centuries, much of the ancient Celtic history was lost - and what is known of their culture has been pieced together from oral traditions passed down through generations and surviving examples of their intricate art.

The ancient Celts were a cluster of tribes who spoke the Celtic languages and lived during the Iron Age. Historians believe the Celts originated from the Hallstatt culture, which can be traced through records and findings from the Bronze and early Iron Ages artifacts. Over time and due to different circumstances, the Celts populated multiple European territories, including modern-day France, Italy, Germany, Poland, Spain, and Britain. After their dissemination, the Celtic tribes were divided into groups such as the Gauls, the Britons, the Gaels, the Celtiberians, the Galatians, and others - creating a great diversity amongst the tribes and making it harder to define their cultural structure. Moreover, the tribes often engaged in warfare with the Romans, who held much of the recorded history of the Celts - but it was colored with biased misunderstanding due to the conflict at the time.

By 300 B.C.E., the Celtic tribes inhabited most of Europe. After the Romans began a campaign against the Celts, and slowly started to destroy many of their civilizations on the mainland of Europe. Initially, the Romans attempted to invade Celtic Britain. However, they could not conquer many of the islands, or the far northern regions, where the Celts had managed to establish their new home. To this day, cultural traditions in Ireland, Scotland, and Wales can be traced back to the ancient Celts.

Celtic traditions still exist in other parts of Europe, including the Asturias region of Northern Spain. The Celts who lived there became the Galatians, and the survival of their traditions in Asturias means that today, they share many cultural commonalities and cultural heritage common with Celtic regions like Ireland and Scotland.

Celtic Societies

In the absence of first-handwritten records, it's almost impossible to discern the exact structure of the ancient Celtic society. That said, from the writing of diligent Roman authors, it can be concluded that Celtic tribes followed a hierarchical system that allowed them to maintain

stability in their communities. This hierarchical system likely had the following classes:
1. **The rulers and elite warriors** - A limited layer of society with many privileges and duties.
2. **Religious leaders and the Druids** - The living repositories of the Celtic community's collective knowledge. They were also exempt from paying taxes or partaking in military service.
3. **The specialized workforce of society.** These included craft workers, farmers, traders, and slaves. This was the largest group comprising less educated individuals.

Another fascinating fact about the Celtic society was how they treated women. Historical evidence suggests that there were several female chiefs in Celtic Britain and many monarchs, as well. These powerful women were responsible for ruling tribes and leading them into battle. In Celtic societies, men and women received equal treatment for elaborate burial rites and offerings. Archeological findings prove that the same amount of possessions depicting high status was buried with male and female leaders of many Celtic tribes.

Iron Age Celtic society was structured around the monarchy. After the society was split into different tribes, each was led by its own king. However, they were also high and low kings - both of which were elected under a tanistry system. The tanistry system was a long-standing custom amongst Celtic tribes, particularly in Ireland and Scotland, but it evolved and eventually changed into the feudal system, which determined the firstborn son as the family successor.

Over time, the ruling system changed to include elected chiefs and officials. Some tribes also had a small council of elders responsible for making the ruling decisions in their community. Often, two or more separate Celtic tribes would merge for mutual assistance and benefit. As a result, one or both of the tribes depended on each other for resources and ruling systems. However, the merger was often necessary due to the impending advancement of the Romans and the threat they posed to the Celts.

Celtic aristocrats used the patronage system they established with their followers to uphold their distinguished and often highly coveted status. They would offer their supporters hospitality, monetary support, different rewards, and legal protection in exchange for labor and the product of this. They were also expected to follow the aristocrats into battle and protect them when necessary. Celts of the highest status had clients from different classes. Sometimes chiefs and kings of lower rank would work with aristocrats with a higher social status and power.

The Celtic monetary system was mostly based on a simple bartering system. This involved exchanging items and services between two or more people without money. While this was a huge part of Celtic society, it also believed that the Celts used some form of proto-money. The Celtic ring money is the most commonly referenced currency among the Iron Age Celts. Gold and copper rings were the common currency in the system using ring money. These rings were often worn on clothing or tied together using ropes to facilitate their exchange of goods and services. Besides the ring money, bronze bells and axe heads also served the purpose of an early currency.

Culture and Religion

Celtic cultural markers varied significantly across the different tribes. All of these tribes were collectively labeled as "Celts," which some modern historians consider problematic because the tribes in the different parts of the world didn't follow a unified tradition. They existed separately in scattered territories, and the Celtic culture spread and evolved with time. It changed most dramatically during the European Iron Age due to their interactions with other cultures and belief systems and continued migrations. Initially, they probably had the same cultural background, beliefs, and customs. However, once they became scattered so widely that the tribes weren't even in direct contact with one another, they had fewer and fewer cultural elements in common.

Historians advise that the Celtic culture originated from three main cultural groups closely related to one another. These groups had the prominent Indo-European facets the Celtic culture (and several other European Pagan cultures) is based on. The first group, the Urnfield culture, can be traced back to the late Bronze Age. They are named after their widespread practice of storing the cremated remains of their dead in urns or burying the urns with the remains. Although there's a lack of archeological evidence proving the existence of this group, this tradition was later widely adopted by Celtic tribes. Ironwork became more prominent after transitioning from the Bronze Age to the Iron Age. This was evidenced in the changes in Celtic culture as well.

Named after the birth site of their original tribe in Upper Austria, the Hallstatt culture quickly scattered through Europe, conquering territories like Switzerland, Austria, Germany, France, and Bohemia. The quick dispersion of this culture across Europe is attributed to factors like trade, marriages, tribal alliances, and migration. It's also known that these tribes had an abundance of salt, iron, and copper deposits – and mastered how to trade these through the waterways. For example, they brought their goods to the Mediterranean and exchanged them for gold and amber jewelry. This is underlined by the amount of these foreign items found in the Hallstatt burial mounds. Unfortunately, due spread of other cultures and tribes and competition, the pool of resources was ultimately depleted, leading to the demise of the Hallstatt culture, which died out at the beginning of the 5th century B.C.E.

The third cultural group linked to the roots of the ancient Celtic culture is the La Tene culture, named after their presumed area of origin in Switzerland. This group of tribes was probably the most diversified of all three cultures. There were, however, some similarities to the other two cultures in art, religion, and language. The influence of the La Tene culture spanned Western and Central Europe, from Ireland to Romania. Several aspects of the everyday life of these groups made their way into the lives of future Celtic tribes, including ironworking, swirling-styled art, offerings made in water, and weapon deposition in tombs.

Among all the later Celtic tribes, the Galatians and the Britons were the two most prominent in establishing the basis of the Celtic culture. The Galatians lived in the Asturias region (northern Spain in modern times). This tribe had successfully fought off invasion attempts from both the Romans and the Moors. The Moors were spreading to the nearby regions at the time and already ruled much of current-day southern Spain. Celtic Galatian traditions have a huge part in Celtic celebrations and rituals. Cultural features of the Galatian tribes resembled earlier Celtic culture a great deal, with many similarities in art and symbolism. For example, the Galatian tribes often partook in traditions involving musical instruments similar to the ones used by Celtic tribes in other parts of Europe, particularly in Ireland and Scotland.

Britons and Gauls, the other two later Celtic tribes, initially settled in Northwestern France (modern-day Brittany). Since they were more isolated than Celts in other parts of Europe, other cultures didn't threaten these tribes, and they managed to retain most of the culture of their ancestors. Many festivals celebrated can be traced back to ancient Celtic customs of honoring nature and deities. While the Romans did not initially manage to invade the Britons, they later succeeded in their attempts, pushing the Britons to the islands near Wales and Cornwall and north to Scotland.

The languages of the ancient Celts stemmed from the Celtic culture. Some of these languages are still in use today, like Welsh. Approximately a million people worldwide speak Welsh, while other languages, like Cornish, have fewer speakers.

Warfare and Craftsmanship

Warfare was deeply entwined in the ancient Celtic art, religion, lifestyle, and social structure. The Celts quickly acquired a warrior reputation among the other cultures in the ancient world. However, much of their barbaric reputation was attributed to them by the Romans, who intended to make the Celts look far scarier and uncivilized than they actually were. Celtic metalworkers used iron, bronze, and gold with tremendous skill, and many of their technological innovations found their way onto the battlefield. Some of the modern metalwork techniques hail from Celtic metalworking. However, when it came to war strategies, the Celtic warriors were less organized than they were portrayed to be by the Romans.

Celtic burials offer a cornucopia of information about the development of their warrior culture. The practice of burying prominent society members with objects related to their status (leaders and wealthier people) and warfare (in the case of warriors) originates from the Celts. Archeological findings have revealed that the Celtic warrior burials can be differentiated from other tombs in prehistoric cemeteries by their elaborate construction and the abundance of additional items they contain.

Celtic warriors were often buried with horse gear and weapons. The archeological findings also indicate that vehicles like carts, chariots, or wagons also found their way into Celtic warrior burial mounds. Sometimes, the buried objects were owned by the deceased in life. At other times, the interment resulted from local beliefs and traditions. For example, placing certain weapons (a sword, a helmet, or a spear) or personal possessions of chieftains had a religious significance for some Celtic tribes.

Across Europe, the Celts were known for their artistic ingenuity and have been credited with creating intricate stone carvings and delicate metal accessories. Creating panoply (armor) was one of the Celtic craftsman's strong suits. As evidenced by archeological findings and Roman writings about the Celts, the ancient Celtic warriors went to battle armed with shields, spears, and swords. Their shields were long and oval to protect vital body parts and often adorned with large bronze or iron bosses (studs in the middle of the shield). The swords, worn on the hip or side, were attached to an iron or bronze chain. The spears used by the Celts varied from lighter ones suitable for direct combat to heavier ones that doubled as lances. Early on, the Celtic armor was fashioned from fabric or leather – only to be replaced by chain mail shirts around the 4th century B.C.E. Chain mails featured tiny interlocking iron circles, which rendered them lighter, allowing the warriors far more freedom of movement. Shirts with broad shoulder straps emerged to help redistribute the chain mail shirt's weight even more. This also added extra protection to the shoulder and back.

Breastplates were also worn among the Celtic warriors in the 6th and 8th centuries B.C.E. There are also records of the Celts using helmets. Despite popular belief, early Celtic headpieces were only used during ceremonies. Instead of protection, they represented a status symbol. Fashioned from expensive and heavy materials like bronze, iron, gold, and coral, it's clear that they were too impractical to be worn during a battle. However, they were all the more suitable for making the wearer stand out in ceremonies. Since Celtic helmets became more practical in the later period, it's presumed that their use was transferred to the battlefield as well.

Celtic Art Symbolism

Celtic art is believed to hail from the much older Indo-European Iron Age. However, some parts of Celtic art can also be traced back to the neighboring nations like the Romans, Greeks, Etruscans, Scythians, and Thracians. Clothes and accessories were the most prominent testimony of Celtic art being featured in everyday life. By the end of the Iron Age, commoners wore long linen or wool trousers (depending on the season) with long-sleeved tunics made from a similar material. However, the wealthy people in society would sometimes have clothing made of silk adorned with intricate designs. In the wintertime, they wore cloaks secured with accessories featuring different symbols. Brooches and armlets were popular at all times of the year. The Celtic torc was probably one of their most prominent accessories, featuring a metal (typically gold) collar around the neck. These were used to identify high-ranking members of society.

The Celts created intricate art pieces in various mediums, from pottery and jewelry to animal figurines and ornate cauldrons. They mostly worked with locally sourced stone, iron, bronze, and gold for the main pieces. While the decorations were made from imported materials like glass, coral, and amber, the decoration depicts symbols that have to be attributed to Celtic traditions.

One of the most renowned Celtic symbols is the Triskele. It depicts three spirals creating a unique rotational symmetry. The triskele is commonly featured in Celtic art and traditions. It's also associated with contemporary Celtic or Pagan traditions. There are several versions of this symbol. For example, the three spirals can be pictured with three bent legs.

The Druids

The Druids were a class of highly educated people within ancient Celtic society. Their ranks included doctors, philosophers, poets, mathematicians, and spiritual leaders. Besides being an elite group, the Druids created a legacy based on the extensive knowledge they've collected over their lifetime. Just like Celtic culture, Druidism was also retained and evolved. Eventually, Druids became associated with magic, mysterious abilities, and deep spiritualism. The history of evolution in the Druidic society followed the development of the Celtic civilization.

Druids were considered an essential part of the Celtic community and were often sought out for their wisdom – to resolve different issues the tribe members or community faced. The word Druid can be traced back to the Latin and Gaulish words "*Druidae*" and "*Druides.*" The word can be broken down into two Celtic words, "*dru*" and "*wid*," which translate as tree and wisdom, respectively. The word reflects the importance of trees in Celtic spiritualism and society. According to other sources, the word druid can also mean magician and sorcerer, a reference to the mystical powers Druids possessed according to the later Celtic societies.

The ancient Druids were classified into a structured hierarchical system based on rank and profession. Each class of Druids had a specific color associated with their status, which also symbolized their role in the Druid system. The eldest and wisest Druids had gold-colored robes. These were known as the *Arch-Druids* and often were approached when a leader had to make a decision that affected their entire community. Ordinary or general Druids wore white robes and usually acted as priests or teachers. Warrior Druids would wear red robes and were also known as sacrificers. Blue robes were worn by artistic Druids classified as bards. The new recruits wore brown or black robes. The different Druid classes had varied life patterns based on the natural cycle they were taught to follow. Among those patterns were following the lunar, solar, and seasonal cycles – and celebrating them with the appropriate events.

Celtic Folklore

Celtic mythology is a fascinating source of folkloric elements emanating from ancient Celtic cultures like the Irish, the Welsh, and the Gauls. Unfortunately, many Celtic myths were only recorded by Roman conquerors during Medieval times, which resulted in them being altered.

That said, it's known that the ancient Celts worshipped a much larger pantheon of deities than their successors. Depending on the location, these gods and goddesses often had different names and features. Some were widely honored by all Celts, while others were only regional deities celebrated in smaller communities.

The Celts' belief in many deities stemmed from the roles each of these gods played. However, the details of the Celtic polytheistic religion are debated because the Celts didn't record their religious practices. Much of the descriptions of these customs come, once again, from Roman literary sources.

Some of the deities of the Celtic pantheon include:

- **Aengus**, the god of love and poetry
- **Badb**, a war goddess
- **Brigid**, the goddess of fertility
- **Cernunnos**, the horned deity
- **Dagda**, the Celtic chief-turned deity
- **Lugh**, the god of justice
- **Morrigan**, another was a goddess/ an aspect of Badb

With some variations across different regions and tribes, components of the ancient Celtic culture included:

- The use of sacred groves, rivers, springs, and other natural sites for ceremonies and rituals involving the reverence of nature, the deities that rule spirits, and other entities.

- Frequent offerings dedicated to different deities, asking for blessings, protection, or healing powers. The offerings included sacrificed animals, weapons, and food items.
- A strong reverence for the afterlife – they often deposited valuables and everyday goods in the deceased's tombs.
- Religious ceremonies were often led by Druids and other highly distinguished tribe members.
- A firm belief in the protective powers of totems, taboos, and sacrifices, especially in times of need.

Chapter 2: Celtic Beliefs and Symbolism

Celtic symbolism can be defined as a set-up of signs and symbols used by the Celts to communicate their beliefs, culture, and spirituality. Besides representing a powerful relationship between signs and ideas, Celtic symbolism is also a unique representation of the Celts' connection to the natural world. From a historical perspective, Celtic symbolism can be traced back to the ancient Celts. Their rich mythology and folklore, and even beyond, to the roots that connect them to other pagan belief systems. Understanding the symbols in the context of Celtic spirituality and paganism can help you see who the ancient Celts were and how they lived their lives. And by looking into these symbols, you can deepen your connection to the natural world, tap into the wisdom of the Celtic tradition, and use it in your day-to-day life.

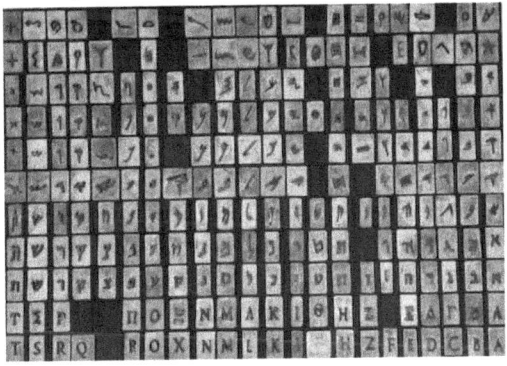

The Celts used symbols and gestures to communicate and spread their culture.[17]

The Celtic Pantheon

The polytheistic belief system of the Celts included reverence for a large number of deities. There are no written records of how these gods and goddesses were worshipped. However, archeological findings provide clues on the variations and commonalities in worship that existed across time and space and between the many ancient Celtic tribes. For example, there is evidence that the Celts often used natural sites like groves, springs, and clearings in elevated spaces to perform rituals and make offerings to their deities.

Nowadays, historians claim that the Celtic pantheon counts more than 400 deities. While some of these beings were at one point imagined as having human-like characteristics, most of them are considered supernatural entities that appear in their own unique form. Some deities worshipped by the Celts were similar to those venerated by other European belief systems. However, the Celts often made them their own by giving them different names while maintaining the same attributes, responsibilities, and powers. Other deities were entirely local – these often appear in the myths of tribes more isolated from the rest of the Celtic tribes and other religions in general. To further complicate the issue, the Celtic deities were given powers and associations that overlapped with those of other gods and goddesses in the Celtic pantheon. That said, these overlapping attributes are unique to the Celtic culture.

Fortunately, Celtic symbolism can also offer further clues about the role of Celtic deities in the cultures of their followers. Inscriptions used for rituals during worship and burial practices suggest that the deities had a powerful hold over people's lives. More often than not, venerating a particular divinity was necessary to maintain the tribe's well-being.

Many gods and goddesses were linked to natural places and phenomena like the sun, water, and lightning – indicating they provided sustenance, healing, and a means of survival. In the times of ancient Celts, finding food and ensuring a plentiful harvest was a well-known concern, and many deities were called upon to assist with hunting in general and even for particular animals like boars and stags and harvest. Others were associated with warfare, families, and tribes and were called upon for protection and guidance to defeat the enemy and preserve people's lives.

One of the most widely revered Celtic deities was Lugh (or Lugus, as he is known by the contemporary Celts), the god of the sun and light.

According to many myths, he is very wise and all-seeing, making him one of the most influential Celtic deities. While he is rarely depicted in art, Lugh has several historic sites and modern-day places named after him. Cerunnos, on the other hand, is a Celtic deity often featured in Celtic symbolism and art. Known as the horned god, Cerunnos is depicted sitting on his magnificent throne, with horns or antlers on his head. His headpiece is a clear indication of his association with his animal nature.

Interestingly, several Celtic deities had triple roles or were viewed as three deities associated with the same natural aspect or facet of life. Some goddesses have names yet represent three different aspects of the same deity. For example, the Celtic pantheon has three mother goddesses depicting fertility, strength, and power. These goddesses were patrons of mothers, children, and Mother Nature. Likewise, other groups like fishermen, metalworkers, and bards have their own patron deities.

Besides having deities looking over certain aspects of nature, the Celts also found it fundamental to worship animals and plants as sacred beings with protective qualities. There is evidence of horses, boars, stags, bulls, and trees appearing as symbols of protection on Celtic armor, weapons, and everyday objects. Animals and plants were considered sacred in real life, too, and any offense to them was punishable – and not only in ancient times. For example, in Ireland, there are six sacred trees.

Celtic amulets offer intricate symbols of nature, making them perfect for the protection of the living and the deceased (as they journey to the Otherworld). Amulets were found in several burial mounds, indicating that those in the burial site had to be protected in the spiritual realm. The most widespread Celtic protective symbols are wheels, shoes, shields, and axes.

Cosmology and Sacred Sites

Much like in its Norse counterpart, the world has three parts in Celtic cosmology – the Sky (Heaven), the Earth, and the Otherworld. At the core of the world is the World Tree, or the Tree of Life, as it is known by the Celts. The tree's highest branches reach Heaven, while its roots go deep into the Otherworld. The latter is surrounded by water, from which the tree gains sustenance. Because of this, the Celts consider bodies of water as gates to the Otherworld. Not only are many burial mounds located near water, but they are also deeply revered worship sites.

The Celts believed springs host supernatural beings like fairies, nymphs, and spirits. The reverence for the springs and its inhabitants is mirrored by archaeological finds associated with the Celts. There are numerous sites where archeologists unearthed stones, animal bones, and Celtic artifacts near springs. Some of these springs are still believed to have curative powers associated with a particular deity. According to legends, lakes were the best places to contact the spirits, gods, and goddesses of the Otherworld. From the archeological findings in several lakes, it can be deduced that people offered sacrifices to the spirits here. There are entire hordes of items people have thrown into lakes in hopes of summoning the spirits. Rivers in places where the ancient Celts lived are often named after Celtic deities associated with powers like protection, healing, and whatever else the Celts required to navigate their lives. Sometimes warriors offered their shields to the gods to honor or appease them because some of the Celtic deities had a volatile nature.

Boglands also have holy aspects, according to the Celts. They are typically associated with protection and supernatural beings like fairies and were often used for rituals and offerings. Some archeological evidence suggests that bogs also served as a final resting place for bards, Druids, and those who delved into magic and other mysterious arts.

Besides consecrated springs, rivers, and bogs, the Celts had other natural sites they considered sacred. Mountains, hilltops, and groves of trees often served as ritual sites. According to oral tradition, the Druids found it particularly conducive to use these sights to gather wisdom and power. Oak is one of the trees the Celts considered sacred. Besides providing shade for people to assemble during rites and ceremonies, the oak trees are also attributed with liminal powers. It represented a connection between this realm and all the other realms – evidenced by the fact that the oak tree is often used to symbolize the Tree of Life in Celtic art.

Some sacred places connected to the earth were entirely natural, while others were man-made. There are several sites where archaeologists found stones and bowls buried in the ground. The latter was likely for collecting offerings and performing animal sacrifices and divinations. Most were found in the open countryside, in clearings, or surrounded by wood. The artificial sacred sites also included stone circles, gates, and similar monuments. In some places, animal bones inside the stones offer evidence that animal sacrifices were made to protect the site and those using it from malicious spiritual influences. The sacred groves used by the

Druids had similar aspects, as they were also man-made and had protective and power-enhancing elements.

Certain sacred places in connection to the Earth also offered a link to the sky. These were higher monuments, either natural, like mountaintops, or man-made. The latter was characteristic of later periods when the Celts began to build temples mimicking other cultures' spiritual and religious traditions. In a natural setting, the man-made natural monuments had only a few artificial elements. For example, people would make an indentation in a natural rock sitting in a clearing and use it for rituals, divination, and other purposes. In Scotland and Ireland, there are several of these sites where Celtic kings are believed to have proclaimed their kingship or addressed people before a battle or other critical event in their lives.

While later on, the Celts began to prepare sacred sites in more urban settings, these places still had a powerful link to nature. Purpose-built monuments on the earth symbolize people's connection to the earth. Whereas shrines and temples were erected to empower their connection to the deities. Megalithic structures erected by earlier civilizations also inspired the Celts to create their own religious sites by transforming the older structure based on their needs. Celtic sacred sites with a rectangular or square clearing surrounded by artificial channels dug into the earth were revealed in Bohemia, France, and southern Germany. The channels represented the perimeter of the site. Some even featured a gate on the east. Historians hypothesize that the bare space in the middle was once filled with strategically placed wooden poles the Celts used to record monumental events. They probably adorned the poles with symbols depicting natural phenomena, people's names and occupations, wars, and more. Others think that some wooden poles acted as supporting beams for temples. Some poles had deep shafts carved into them for votive offerings. Archeological findings from the 2nd and 1st centuries B.C.E. indicate that the Celts also used items made with pottery and metalwork in sacrificial sites. These items had symbols associated with deities, spirits, and the natural world.

The oldest Celtic stone temples were built in the 4th century B.C.E. These featured spacious doorways adorned with early Celtic symbols. Their roof was often made of intertwining branches (referencing the Celtic reverence toward the trees) held together with clay and lime. The Celtic belief about the soul residing in the head was also showcased with the ornate masks Celts used to decorate their ancient temples. After being conquered by the Romans, Celts shifted to erecting temples featuring classical Roman architectural elements. However, they found a way to give homage to the ancient gods with featureless adornments covered in metal torcs. Before that, it was rare for the Celts to depict deities through stone monuments. If they did, these were simple standing stone pillars or carvings made into domes adorned with the representations of the head (and, through it, the soul) and nature. The latter was depicted via symbols of plants, trees, and other vegetal designs.

Symbolism in Rituals and Offerings

Celtic rituals are often held to honor nature, the spirits and the afterlife, and the deities. Rites that follow the schedule based on nature's cycles, the Moon's phases, and other heavenly bodies offer a powerful connection to these elements. Each had a cyclical nature, which the Celts associated with the cycle of life.

Incantations and prayers were recited to the deities, and votive offerings were made to them since ancient times. Sometimes, the symbolism of the deity worship was tied to other beliefs. For example, in Scotland and Ireland, there are several sites where places of worship and ritual were erected near burial mounds. In these places, several mounds represent the graves of important individuals whose power could have been used to empower rituals and ceremonies. These places still have visitors that leave small offerings in the hope of obtaining empowerment, guidance, or recovery from ailments.

Interestingly enough, unlike the objects found in the burial grounds, the items in the worship sites appeared to be broken. It is believed that this was the Celt's way of denouncing the object and stating that it now belonged to the god, goddess, or spirit they offered it to.

While Roman and other literary sources suggest that human sacrifice was practiced among the ancient Celts, there is little evidence of whether this was true or simply Rome's way of making the Celts look more barbaric. Animal sacrifices were common, but even these rituals have been discarded over the centuries. Whether ancestors were buried or burned, contemporary Celtic pagans only offered animal parts they would discard after preparing the rest for a meal.

Besides protection, ancient Celts also used animal sacrifices for divination. Different animal parts were associated with district aspects of life, and based on this, they offered clues about the future events in these aspects.

A unique form of offering was the burial of items. They were often buried in shallow ground after being offered precious goods for a cause. Several objects (like torcs, coins, and necklaces) were tied together or covered with a piece of fabric before being deposited into the ground. Items were often offered and buried on the same site (not in the same pit but others nearby) over many years. The number of items found in these places implies that the area was considered sacred. Despite initially viewing them as safety deposits, historians now agree they were part of an ancient Celtic ritual. The sites were likely associated with a deity, a protective or healing aspect of nature, or represented a liminal space.

When it comes to the unique Celtic burial mounds, these were tied to the Celts' deep reverence towards the afterlife. Celtic pagan traditions affirm that when a person dies in this world, their soul travels to the Otherworld. However, when one person dies, another is born, and their soul emerges to the earth. Sometimes, those who journeyed to the Otherworld stay there to act as spiritual guides and protectors, particularly during the liminal periods. By burying their dead in natural sites, the ancient Celts symbolically gave them back to the earth where they came from. The items buried with them helped grant a safe journey and gain the assistance of the gods of the Otherworld.

Other Prominent Symbolism in Celtic Culture

Besides the movement of the moon, sun, and other heavenly bodies, ancient Celtic cosmology revolved around symbolism, including spirals and wheels. Both of these are linked to the never-ending cycle of life. The seasons turned each year like points on a giant wheel - hence many Celtic pagans followed and still followed a calendar called the Wheel of the Year.

The symbolism of the stars is tied to the belief in the North Star, the axis of the sky - which also represented the gates of the heavens. According to Celtic mythology, as the stars moved around this axis, they formed a spiral path.

The continuous spirals are also tied to the Celtic belief that when one cycle ends, another commences. The seemingly endless expansion of the spiral might also denote that wisdom can be grown too. Triplicate symbols are said to be attributed to divine empowerment.

Since the ancient Celts based their calendar on the moon's cycles, their year had 13 months. Twelve are similar to the months in modern calendars, while the 13th has only three days and only acted as a guide for those preparing for the coming year. Additionally, each month has a sacred Ogham tree linked to it.

Each of the four seasons was celebrated with a specific holiday, marking a momentous occasion in people's lives. Samhain, which marks the beginning of the winter and the cessation of hunting and harvesting, and Beltane, the festival that welcomes the summer and the beginning of true life in nature, are both traditionally celebrated with fire. During these periods, the veil between the worlds becomes thinner, allowing spirits from the Otherworld to come to and fro, sending and carrying messages. Imbolc and Lughnasadh are two other fire festivals observing events like Solstices and Equinoxes. Several ritual sites are built in a way that they align with these points on the Wheel of the Year.

Around the festivals, the Celts were even more fascinated by the liminal spaces, like doorways and shorelines, and considered them places of empowerment. They would often gather on the shore where they could make a connection between the solid, material world and the fluid spiritual world. The festivals also provide a fantastic opportunity for the Celts to approach their deities and ancestors.

Tree of Life

This symbol is frequently featured in art and used widely in Celtic rituals, ceremonies, or ways of life in general. Nowadays, you can see it in jewelry, talismans, and even tattoos. However, its significance goes much deeper than being an aesthetically pleasing design. The Tree of Life represented a connection to the natural world for thousands of years. Given that trees are always a vital source of food, shelter, firewood, and medicine for humanity, it's easy to see why a tree may have a significant symbolism in the Celtic culture.

It's believed that the Druids played a fundamental role in giving trees spiritual significance. Besides using them for rituals and worship, they also knew that trees (especially the oak) were a great place to look for mistletoe – a tree with spiritually empowering effects.

After arriving on new territory, ancient Celtic tribes often settled around a tree (like an oak), which acted as a central point for community activities like rituals and ceremonies. The Celts believed that forming the settlement around the tree granted the community wisdom, strength, and longevity. If you are wondering why oaks were the most common trees used for this purpose, the answer lies in their longevity. The lifespan of an

Oak tree can reach up to several hundred years.

Other trees used as focal points or places of worship near a community were yews – which live even longer, for thousands of years. To this day, the Celts also believe that given that roots of the trees extend deep into the ground, this symbolizes the connection between the Tree of Life and the Otherworld. They use trees to connect with their ancestors.

Chapter 3: A-Z of Celtic Symbols

This chapter delves into the interpretations and spiritual meanings of various symbols found in Celtic mythology, folklore, and spirituality.

Ailm

Ailm is a symbol of flexibility and maturity.

This symbol comes from the first letter of Ogham, believed to have been the earliest form of written communication in Celtic Ireland. It is a symbol of an evergreen conifer, known as silver fir. People at the time referred to a particular group of trees as the Ogham because they thought these conifers had an indispensable amount of wisdom to share. In Celtic mythology, evergreens have powerful healing powers and can revitalize the human soul. Ailms are symbols of flexibility, rehabilitation, maturity, strength, resilience, and inner power.

Awen

Awen represents the virtues of truth, love, and wisdom.[18]

The Awen symbol is also referred to as the "Three Rays of Light" because it's shown as three circles, each representing sources or centers of light, with a ray extending from each. A renowned Welsh poet was the first to mention this neo-Druid symbol during the 18th century. Researchers, however, suggest that the invention of the Awen goes back further.

The term "Awen" translates to "essence" or "inspiration," which is why there are various interpretations of what the symbol stands for. Some practitioners believe that the three rays are representative of the essence of life; air, sea, and earth. Others suggest they symbolize the essence of humans or mind, body, and spirit. According to some interpretations, the three rays are symbols of the most important virtues of truth, love, and wisdom.

Truthfulness, compassion, and understanding are the three cornerstones of awakening and are believed to be represented by the three rays. Many people think that reinvigoration and the state of being present and conscious come from inspiration. Awakening, however, goes hand-in-hand with the truth. You can't seek the truth if you're not awake.

Simpler interpretations of the symbol suggest that the Awen represents the ability of opposite forces to exist harmoniously in the universe. Masculine and feminine energies are depicted as the left and right rays, while the middle ray symbolizes the harmony and balance maintained between both energies.

Beltane

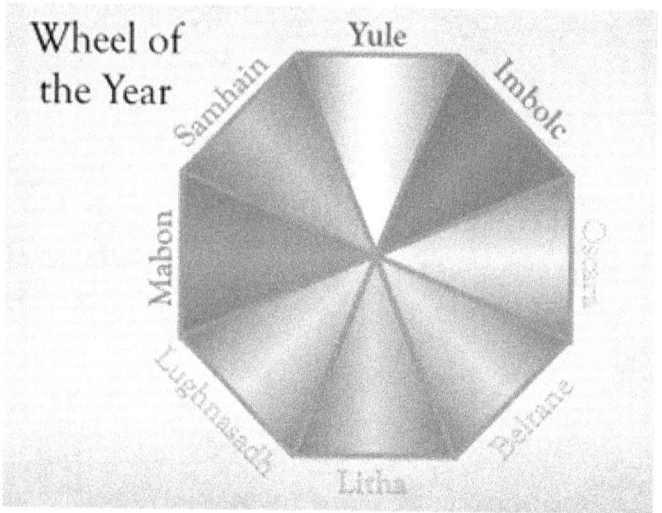

The wheel of the year.[19]

The Wheel of the Year is a Celtic calendar that revolves around eight seasonal festivals: Imbolc, Ostara, Beltane, Litha, Lughnasa, Mabon, Samhain, and Yule. Each of the eight sabbats, or festivals, has its own symbol. Beltane is celebrated on May 1st to welcome summer, and people pray to the deities for abundance in crops and good weather. This celebration falls right between the spring equinox and the summer solstice.

Brigid's Cross

This symbol is among the oldest Celtic Irish emblems and can be traced to the goddess Brigid in the Celtic myth Tuatha de Danaan. Many suggest this deity was later transfigured into the Christian saint of Kildare after the religion made its way into Ireland. Practitioners believe they can invoke the saint's or goddess' protective energies if they hang this symbol on their doors or in the corridors.

A Brigid's Cross is made out of straws and rushes.[20]

Straw and rushes are conventionally used to weave the cross on the Sabbat Imbolc, which is the day that celebrates the goddess Brigid. According to lore, this symbol was initially gifted to her father on his deathbed. The goddess' father knew that the cross was a holy symbol, which is why he felt the need to be baptized and die in purity.

Bowen Knot

The loops in a Bowen knot symbolize true love, loyalty, and flowing water.[21]

Celtic knots are patterns of loops and knots that have symbolic meanings. That they have neither a beginning nor an end symbolizes the infinite nature of life. Celtic knots can be traced back to the 8th century and have been used by practitioners to decorate their spaces and bring certain energies into their lives. Each Celtic pattern or knot symbolizes different virtues or emotions and has unique interpretations.

The Bowen knot comes in different forms. The two most common are a square with four outward-pointing loops at each corner or a cross with four pointy loops at each end. These loops symbolize true love, loyalty, and flowing water.

Celtic Spiral

Spirals are emblems of spiritual growth and development.[22]

According to Celtic mythology, spirals are emblems of spiritual growth and development. Spirals are also symbols of energy constantly emitted from human bodies and their surroundings. They also represent space and the infinite nature of the universe. The Celtic spiral suggests that humans are always in a state of evolution and experiencing balance among their minds, bodies, and spirits.

They are often used to decorate spaces and are depicted in various forms to convey certain meanings. A single spiral that rotates counterclockwise represents human growth and development throughout life. A single spiral that rotates clockwise is representative of water and movement.

Double spirals symbolize the dual nature of all existence, representing the balance between two contrasting forces. Wet and dry, feminine and masculine, and night and day, for example, can all be represented by double spirals. The duality of nature is needed to maintain balance and harmony. A double spiral which is centered is an emblem of harmony and the moon. A combined double spiral symbolizes different directions.

Cernunnos

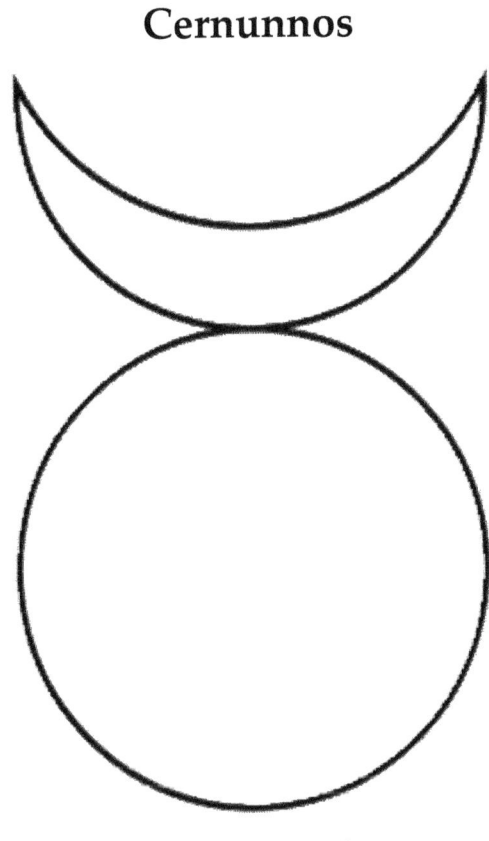

Cernunnos symbol.[23]

The ancient Celts considered Cernunnos one of the most important deities in the pantheon, which is why his symbol remains one of the most popular. He is the god of life, animal, fertility, and wild animals. He is also the underworld deity and is associated with the natural cycle of death and rebirth. Cernunnos is often illustrated sitting cross-legged with antlers on his head, and his symbol is a circle with an upward-facing crescent, symbolizing a horned head.

Circular Knots

Circular knots can come in this pattern.[24]

Circular knots come in various patterns and sizes, depending on the energy the user wishes to bring into their life. Circular knots mainly symbolize inner life, the infinite nature of life, the cycle of life, and the sun.

Cross of Triquetras

The Cross of Triquetras is also referred to as the Carolingian Cross.[25]

The Cross of Triquetras, also known as the Carolingian Cross, symbolizes motherhood, virginity, purity, and wisdom. These virtues are considered the three aspects of the goddess. This Celtic symbol is also associated with the rotation of the sun and its position in the sky (sunset, sunrise, zenith, etc.). Some historical accounts suggest that this symbol was also used as an emblem for the male trinity.

Dara Celtic Knot

The Dara knot takes the shape of an oak tree's roots.

The term "*Dara*" is derived from an ancient Celtic word that means "oak." This is why the symbol takes the intricate shape of an old oak tree's roots. Like all the other Celtic knots, the Dara knot has neither a beginning nor an end. Oak trees were sacred to the Celts because they were associated with their deities and played significant roles in ancient Celtic legends. They were also places of worship and were believed to be gateways to the otherworld. Oak trees were believed to be sources of knowledge and wisdom, which is why people often turned to them for guidance. The oak tree is a source of nourishment and inner strength, and wisdom.

Druid Sigil

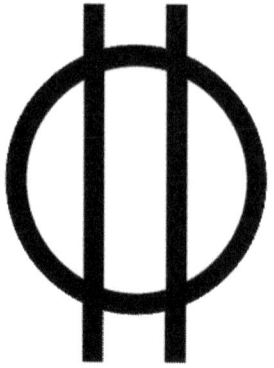

The Druid Sigil.[26]

A Druid Sigil takes the shape of a circle and has two lines that look like tree branches inside. Sigils are commonly used in ritual magic and symbolize fertility, reproduction, and Mother Nature.

Eostre

Eostre, also known as Ostara, is celebrated on the spring equinox, usually on March 20th in the northern hemisphere. Practitioners celebrate Ostara because it symbolizes the balance between two extreme weathers (summer and winter) and light and dark because the day is equally split between daytime and nighttime during the equinox. This festival is considered the predecessor of modern-day Easter.

Eternity Knot

The eternity knot is important in many religions and cultures.[27]

The eternal knot is an important symbol in many religions and cultures around the world, including Buddhism, Jainism, Hinduism, Tibet, Buryatia, and Mongolia. The Celtic eternity knot looks unique and is generally the most popular. The knot has a beautiful design symbolizes eternity, love, and romantic and non-romantic relationships.

Five-Fold Symbol

The five-fold symbol represents spirituality and faith.

While this is among the lesser-known Celtic emblems, the five-fold symbol is one of the most significant. The five interwoven circles of the emblem symbolize the five traditional Celtic basic elements of the universe. The emblem also represents spirituality, God, faith, and heaven, or the four cardinal directions. The fifth ring, in either case, symbolizes harmony, balance, or the universe.

Imbolc

Imbolc, which is also referred to as St. Brigid's Day, takes place on February 1st. This festival marks the beginning of spring and is right between the Winter solstice and the spring equinox. Practitioners celebrate Imbolc because this is when light or sunshine returns.

Litha

This sabbat is celebrated between the 20th and 23rd of June, marking midsummer or the summer solstice in the northern hemisphere. Litha is also the longest day of the year and is celebrated for its agricultural fertility and abundance.

Lughnasadh

This is a Gaelic festival that takes place on August 1st, marking the start of the harvest season. This festival is named after the Celtic deity Lughnasadh, the deity of harvest, agriculture, and livestock, and it is celebrated in his honor.

Mabon

Mabon is celebrated on the Autumnal Equinox between the 21st and 24th of September. Like Eostre, this holiday celebrates balance and harmony in the universe. This day is perfectly split between day and night.

Quaternary Celtic Knot

Quaternary knots protect users from negative energy.

Knots with four loops weren't very common among ancient Celts because they preferred using circular knots or ones with three loops. Quaternary knots, however, are still very popular because they help protect their users from negative energy. This knot is a symbol of groundedness and support. It offers a sense of peace, confidence, and stability.

Samhain

This sabbat is celebrated on November 1st, marking the start of winter and the end of the harvesting season. As Eostre is the predecessor of Easter, Samhain is believed to be the forerunner of Halloween. This holiday is connected to the ancestors and the world of the dead.

The Bird

Birds were believed to be the messengers of the gods.[28]

Animals played a significant role in the ancient Celtic life. Celts used to inscribe symbols of the animals on their amulets and ornaments to bring specific energy and meanings into their lives. They used images of birds to symbolize freedom and bridge the gap between Earth and the heavens. Birds were believed to be the messengers of the gods.

The Boar

Boards represent both stubbornness and the kindness of women.[39]

This animal had two distinct meanings in the ancient Celtic world. It stood for stubbornness, persistence, and strength of warriors. It was also associated with the hospitality and kindness of women. People enjoyed its meat as a delicacy.

The Bull

The Celts considered bulls sacred.[80]

Depictions of bulls were used to decorate nearly every ancient Celtic home. This animal was considered sacred and was venerated by all. The bull is thought to be a symbol of prosperity and fertility, which is why people wanted to bring its energy into their homes.

The Cauldron

The Cauldron was a symbol of well-being.[81]

The Cauldron symbolized well-being and was associated with feasting and matters of the dead. Ancient Celts incorporated large cauldrons into their funerary rites and believed that they were vessels that transported the dead to the otherworld. The Cauldron was also viewed as a symbol of rebirth and abundance. Some featured a cauldron that could feed hundreds of soldiers and revive dead warriors.

The Celtic Cross

The Celtic Cross represents the elements and directions.[82]

This widespread Gaelic symbol incorporates a circle with a cross in the center. This emblem is representative of the elements and the directions. This symbol's sense of continuity symbolizes the eternal development of humans. Practitioners believed that carrying this symbol around would give them knowledge and guidance, and protect them from unwanted forces, as it combines the Christian symbol of the cross and the Celtic symbol of the sun.

The Claddagh Ring

The Claddagh ring is a symbol of marriage and love.[33]

This ring is named after the island on which it was created. The Claddagh ring is a Celtic symbol of marriage, love, and romantic and non-romantic relationship. The ring comprises a heart, which resembles love, and a crown on top of it, which is an emblem of loyalty. Wearing the heart on one's finger symbolizes protection, guidance, and support.

The Deer

Deers are associated with the Tree of Life.[34]

The deer is associated with the Tree of Life because it represents the unity of the universe. The animal is a symbol of strength, and its horns, characterized by their ability to regrow, signify the power of nature. Ancient Celts drew on the energy of this animal to grow and revitalize their spirituality.

The Green Man

The Green Man is a symbol of rebirth.[35]

The Green Man is a symbol of rebirth and is associated with spring. Some ancient Celts believed that this figure was the protector of the forest. According to some historical accounts, this symbol was eminent in several legends across different cultures. The Green Man was particularly important to Celtic tradition because they believed that nature was sacred, were largely concerned about the fertility of their lands, and viewed abundant harvest as a sign of prosperity.

The Sailor's Knot

The sailor's knot symbolizes the undying nature of true love.

The strong and intricate weaving of the sailor's knot symbolizes true love's perseverance and undying nature, regardless of how far away loved ones are. This symbol shows that true love holds out against rough waves and storms, representing all the obstacles that come with life. Sailors used to give these symbols in the form of amulets to their wives before they sailed off to remind them of their undying love. Sailors also kept the Sailor's Knot with them because they thought it had protective energies and attracted food fortune. They believed that carrying it around would keep the weather stable and protect and guide them throughout their journey.

The Shamrock

The shamrock was considered protection from negative energy.[56]

This is the most popular Irish symbol to this day. Celtic Lore suggests that St. Patrick explained the concept of the Trinity by pulling the shamrock from the earth. The Celts used this symbol to protect themselves from the evil eye, malice, and negative energies. It was also used to attract prosperity and good fortune.

The Tree of Life

This symbol looks like an encircled tree with hands reaching upward for branches. The roots are shaded and connected to the hands. This symbol is representative of the harmony and unity between the terrestrial, the underground, and the heavens. Celts believed trees were sacred beings and served as portals to the spirits, the heavens, and the ancestors.

Triquetra

Triquetra symbolizes the nature of life.[87]

Ancient Celts believed that important things came in threes, which is why the Triquetra is considered one of the most important Celtic symbols. It comprises endless loops that symbolize the nature of life, beginning from birth to rebirth. The Triquetra is also associated with the Holy Trinity in Christianity.

Triskeles

This symbol represents the unity of the three elements of fire, earth, and water. It is formed of three spirals and is believed to be the oldest symbol of spirituality. Triskeles are symbols of the cycle of life or birth, death, and the rebirth that follows. It is also associated with the harmony between the mental, physical, and spiritual aspects of the self. The symbol communicates the message that all that is important in the world come in sets of three.

Wheel of Taranis

The Wheel of Taranis symbolizes the wheel of a ship.[38]

This symbol represents the wheel of a ship and is associated with the deities, the basic elements, the sun, and the sky. It is named after the Celtic god of thunder, Taranis. The deity is often depicted holding a wheel in one hand and a lightning bolt in the other.

Yule

Yule is celebrated between December 21st and January 1st, marking the winter solstice – the midpoint of winter. Practitioners anticipate the New Sun and the positivity and abundance it would bring to Earth.

Chapter 4: The Celtic Tree Calendar

Many ancient cultures were fascinated with astrology. They were curious to find how the stars' movements or the sun's positions could influence someone's personality and future. The ancient Celts were no different and had a huge interest in Zodiac signs. However, they had their own interpretation of astrology.

Unlike the Gregorian calendar, the Celtic tree system was based on the lunar cycle. Ancient humans used the Moon as a method to tell time and determine the days, weeks, and months. The Celts went through various experiments and rituals to understand how the lunar cycle worked until they developed their own unique system.

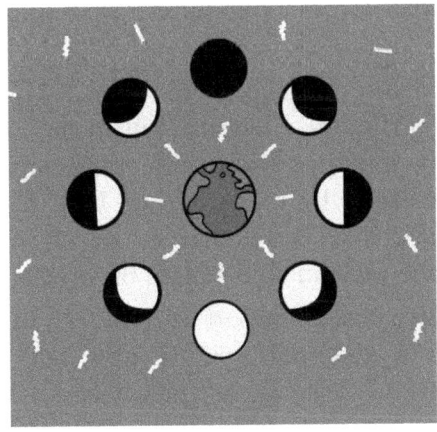

The Celts based their tree system on the lunar cycle.[89]

The calendar is divided into thirteen months, and each is linked to a tree associated with Celtic mythology and an Ogham alphabet (the ancient Irish alphabet that will be discussed in detail in the next chapter). These sacred trees are associated with magic, healing, elements, and deities.

This chapter covers the Celtic tree calendar and its origin and will provide detailed information about its zodiac signs.

The History and Mythology of the Celtic Tree Calendar

There have been many disagreements among scholars about the origin of the Celtic tree calendar. Some believe that it wasn't the ancient Celts who invented it but author and poet Robert Graves, a student of Irish and Celtic mythology. He created this system in 1948, making it a modern invention. He was influenced by the tree calendar that the Druids designed centuries ago.

Graves used the ancient "Song of Amergin" to create his system. The Song of Amergin is one of the oldest poems in the world. However, it is shrouded with mystery since no one knows who wrote it or when and where it was written. Graves believed the song was written in 1268 BC in the British Isles. He translated it and adapted the fifteen consonants of the ancient Ogham alphabet to thirteen letters to correspond with the thirteen lunar cycles that take place each year. Graves divided the calendar into thirteen months with twenty-eight days each and added an extra day to make the year 365 days.

The belief that Graves was the one who created the Celtic tree calendar is common among many scholars because no evidence suggests the Celts ever used this system.

Graves introduced the calendar in his book "The White Goddess," which focused on Middle Eastern, European, Irish, and British mythology. Since not much is known about the ancient Druids or the Celts, Graves was inspired by the works of Irish historian Ruaidhrí Ó Flaithbheartaigh. Ruaidhrí covered the history of Ireland, including its legends, myths, and the Ogham alphabet, in his books.

Whether all credit goes to Robert Graves or not, he wouldn't have been able to develop his system without the Druids laying the groundwork for him. He also based his work on Celtic folklore and mythology and combined it with modern discoveries and beliefs to create this brilliant calendar.

While other scholars agree that the Druids created this system, some modern Celtic pagans believe that the tree calendar existed before the Druids rose to power and became the most influential religious group among the Celts. Many scholars are inclined to believe that the tree system existed before the Druids, but they were the ones who improved on it and discovered the magical properties of each sacred tree.

Simply put: the system that existed before the Druids were the foundation they based their work on to create the Celtic tree calendar - still used today.

The sacred trees associated with the thirteen months have an interesting mythology behind them. The Druids believed that all mankind was the descendants of trees. Each one also symbolizes a Celtic god or goddess and has its own meaning and characteristics that influence the people born under its month. This resembles the concept of Zodiac signs that believe that the sun's position on the day you were born impacts your personality.

The Celtic Tree Zodiac

The Celtic tree zodiac is a system of astrology based on the ancient Celtic reverence for trees. The trees were considered sacred, believed to hold wisdom and power, and associated with particular qualities and characteristics. Each tree has its ruling planet, animal, gemstone, color, Ogham letter, and more. This zodiac system is more complex than Western and Chinese astrology because the Druids spent years studying trees. The ancient Celts predicted the future by listening to the leaves as they whispered their secrets to them. They also used the Ogham alphabet and the lunar cycles to determine people's characteristics.

The Tree Calendar and the Natural World

Nature has always been fascinating and piqued the interest of all poets and authors. Many stories and poems take place around nature, especially in the woods hence the terms magical or enchanted forest. Before the invention of medicine, plants, and herbs provided a remedy to all ailments, whether physical or mental.

Trees are the most majestic part of nature, they are powerful, unique, and old, and life would be impossible without them.

The ancient and Neo-Druids revere trees and would hold their ceremonies and meditate under them. The word "Druid" also means "the knowledge of the oak." They considered trees to be living beings capable of experiencing various emotions and connecting the Earth to the Heavens.

The Druids chose to associate their calendar with trees because they believed nature to be sacred. Trees also change colors during the seasons, making them the perfect representation of the cycle of nature and the changing seasons.

The tree calendar determines the festivals the ancient and neo-pagans celebrate to mark the beginning of each season. For instance, the Samhain festival celebrates the beginning of winter, and Ostara marks the beginning of spring. These festivals will be discussed in detail in the coming chapter.

Now that you understand the history and mythology behind the Celtic tree calendar, the second part of the chapter will focus on the thirteen sacred trees and what they represent.

Birch Moon (December 24 – January 20)

Elements

Air and water.

Seasons

Spring and fall.

Ruling Planet

Venus.

Color

White.

Gemstone

Crystal.

Animals

White stag and golden eagle.

Ogham Letter

Beith (B).

Symbolism

Regeneration, new beginnings, growth, and rebirth.

Correspondence
Capricorn.
Mythology
In Celtic mythology, the Birch tree symbolizes love. Ancient Celts placed their branches over newborns' cribs to protect them from harm and evil spirits.
Deity
Eostre, the goddess of spring.
Zodiac
People born under the birch tree are driven, goal-oriented, and ambitious. They are constantly working on developing themselves in various areas of their lives. Since these individuals are born during the darkest time of the year, they constantly look for the light in themselves and others. They are capable of finding beauty wherever they go. They are charming individuals who are always smiling and patient with others. Yet, they can be strong and tough leaders.

Rowan Moon (January 21 – February 17)

Element
Fire.
Seasons
Spring and fall.
Ruling Planet
The Sun.
Color
Gray.
Gemstone
Peridot.
Animal
Dragon.
Ogham Letter
Luis (L).
Symbolism
Connection, protection, and courage.

Correspondences
Pisces and Aquarius.

Mythology
The Celts associated this tree with success, power, and personal growth. They used to carve a charm on its twig and wear it for protection. Some cultures planted this tree in graveyards so the spirits of the dead wouldn't linger in the world of the living but would cross to the other side.

Deity
Brighid, the goddess of home and fertility.

Zodiac
People born under this sign are unique individuals. They have a vision and goals they work hard to achieve. Although they may seem cool and aloof on the outside, they are extremely passionate and energetic on the inside. They often have creative ideas and a wide imagination. People can find them intimidating because they can have a tough exterior. However, they are kind and caring individuals who are supportive of others.

Ash Moon (February 18 – March 17)

Elements
Fire and water.

Seasons
Spring and fall.

Ruling Planets
Neptune and the Sun.

Color
Green.

Gemstone
Coral.

Animals
Seagull, seahorse, and seal.

Ogham Letter
Nion (N).

Symbolism
Power, growth, and leadership.

Correspondences
Aries and Pisces.

Mythology
The Ash tree is one of the highly revered trees among the Celts and is considered the forest's queen. They used its wood to protect them from the fairies and its seeds to perform divination. In some places in Scotland, people used parts of the tree for protection against dark magic. Some Druids used its wood to make their wands. In Norse mythology, the Yggdrasil, the world tree and the center of the universe, was an Ash tree.

Deity
Odin, the Norse god of war and death.

Zodiac
People born under this tree are shy introverts who enjoy spending time alone. This makes them seem mysterious, and many people find them intriguing. When you get to know them, you will find that they are creative individuals with attractive personalities. They don't concern themselves with anything superficial and are often focused on their inner world and vision. They are confident and never bother with other people's opinions about them.

Alder Moon (March 18 – April 14)

Elements
Water and fire.

Season
Spring.

Ruling Planet
Mars.

Color
Red.

Gemstone
Ruby.

Animals
Hawk, fox, and bear.

Ogham Letter
Fearne (F).

Symbolism
Passion, peace, protection, healing, confidence, and determination.

Correspondences
Aries and Pisces.

Mythology
Alder is the tree of wisdom, and it is favored by all the fairies. Bran the Blessed, the mythical king of Britain, used the wood of the Alder to protect him during battle.

Deity
Bran, the god of regeneration.

Zodiac
These people are strong leaders. They are outgoing, charming, and warm individuals who get along with everyone they meet. Others gravitate towards them because they find their confidence infectious. Passionate individuals, they are always working on something, whether to advance in their careers or improve their lives. They prefer to have deep conversations than discuss the weather.

Willow Moon (April 15 – May 12)

Elements
Earth and air.

Seasons
Winter and summer.

Ruling Planet
The Moon.

Color
Yellow.

Gemstone
Moonstone.

Animals
Sea serpent and hare.

Ogham Letter
Saille (S).
Symbolism
Regeneration, fertility, and flexibility.
Correspondences
Taurus and Gemini.
Mythology
The willow tree is associated with growth and healing. The Celts planted it near their homes to protect them against natural disasters.
Deity
Donn, the god of death.
Zodiac
These people are genuine, honest, kind, sympathetic, generous, and decent. They lead quiet lives and steer clear of drama. They are intelligent, loving, peaceful, and have the ability to read others. They are polite individuals who treat everyone with respect. People born under this sign have a great sense of humor and always spread joy wherever they go.

Hawthorn Moon (May 13 – June 9)
Elements
Air and water.
Seasons
Spring and fall.
Ruling Planets
Venus and Mars.
Color
Purple.
Gemstone
Topaz.
Animals
Owl and bee.
Ogham Letter
Huathe (H).

Symbolism
Marriage and purification.
Correspondences
Gemini and cancer.
Mythology
This tree is associated with protection and love. The Celts referred to it as the "Fairy Tree" because these magical creatures guard it. Hence, the people considered it to be sacred and treated it with love and respect.
Deity
Eostre, goddess of spring.
Zodiac
People born under this sign are creative and passionate. Mature individuals, they are prepared to deal with whatever the universe throws at them. Whenever they find someone in trouble, they never hesitate to lend a helping hand. Trustworthy individuals, people often gravitate towards them when they need to vent or share their secrets. They have the ability to see the bigger picture in every situation and deal with all their problems with a big smile.

Oak Moon (June 10 – July 7)

Element
Water.
Season
Summer.
Ruling Planets
Mars and Jupiter.
Color
Black.
Gemstone
Diamond.
Animals
Horse, otter, and wren.
Ogham Letter
Duir (D).

Symbolism
Caring, intuition, strength, and wisdom.
Correspondences
Cancer and Leo,
Mythology
The Celts considered the Oak tree to be the king of the forest. It is associated with myths, rituals, and religion. The Druids revered it highly and held their meetings and rituals under its protection.

In an ancient Celtic legend, there was a king called Math Mathonwy whose dear nephew Lleu Llaw Gyffes was under a terrible curse that prevented him from marrying a human woman, so the king enlisted the help of a sorcerer who went by the name Gwydion to create a beautiful woman for Lleu to marry.

However, she wasn't a real person and never had a normal life which made her weak, and she quickly gave in to temptation. She had an affair with another man, and they both agreed to kill her husband.

Blodeuwedd and her lover attacked Lleu, and he was wounded. He transformed into an eagle and sought refuge in an oak tree until a sorcerer came and cured him. From this day, the oak tree was known as a place for protecting the weak.

Deity
Thor, the Norse god of thunder
Zodiac
These people speak up for those who can't defend themselves. They are patient, calm, generous, and optimistic individuals who believe that things can always get better no matter how bad their circumstances are right now. They are social creatures who are always surrounded by their loved ones.

Holly Moon (July 8 – August 4)

Elements
Water and fire.
Seasons
Summer.

Ruling Planet
Earth.
Color
Silver.
Gemstone
Carnelian.
Animals
Unicorn and cat.
Ogham Letter
Tinne (T).
Symbolism
Optimism, strength, and protection.
Correspondences
Cancer and Leo.
Mythology
The ancient Celts used the wood of the Holly tree in protective spells and to attract good fortune.
Deity
Thor, the god of thunder.
Zodiac
These people are noble individuals who treat others with respect. They are strong and confident, which makes them natural-born leaders. Failure never discourages them. On the contrary, it motivates them to keep going until they achieve their goals. They are warm, kind, and genuine but are often reluctant to let others see this side of them.

Hazel Moon (August 5 – September 1)

Elements
Fire and Earth.
Seasons
Summer.
Ruling Planet
Mercury.

Color
Brown.
Gemstone
Amethyst.
Animals
Salmon and crane.
Ogham Letter
Coll (C).
Symbolism
Divination, knowledge, intuition, and uniqueness.
Correspondences
Leo and Virgo.
Mythology
In Celtic mythology, the fairies lived in the hazel tree, and many people believed its wood to be sacred. They used it for magic and divination. In one legend, the Irish poet Finn Eces was intrigued by the ancient salmon of knowledge. One day, he decided to catch it and feed it to Fionn Mac Cumhaill, the most famous hero in Irish mythology. The fish had acquired his knowledge from eating nuts from the hazel tree and passed it to Fionn.
Zodiac
Quiet individuals, these people prefer to spend time with themselves than in crowds. They are smart and knowledgeable and know how to solve any problem that comes their way. Loyal and sympathetic, their friends can always count on them.

Vine Moon (September 2 – September 29)
Elements
Air and Earth.
Season
Fall.
Ruling Planet
Venus.

Color

Pastel colors.

Gemstone

Emerald.

Animals

Swan, hound, and lizard.

Ogham Letter

Muin (M).

Symbolism

Endurance, opportunity, change, and reward.

Correspondences

Virgo and Libra.

Mythology

In Celtic mythology, the vine tree was a symbol of emotion, initiation, and wisdom. People used its leaves to boost their ambition.

Zodiac

People born under this sign love to be surrounded by beauty. They believe that being better people will benefit them and their community. They have an expensive taste and enjoy spoiling themselves. However, they work hard to support their luxurious lifestyle and share their gifts with the people in their lives. They prefer to stay neutral during disagreements and avoid confrontations.

Ivy Moon (September 30 – October 27)

Elements

Water and air.

Season

Fall.

Ruling Planet

The Moon.

Color

Blue.

Gemstone

Opal.

Animals
Goose, butterfly, and boar.
Ogham Letter
Gort (G).
Symbolism
Love, new opportunities, renewal, and growth.
Correspondences
Libra and Scorpio.
Mythology
The Celts performed rituals to Arianrhod at the ivy tree to open the portal to the underworld, which is also called "the dark side of the moon." Hence, it became a symbol of the mystical and mysterious.
Deity
Arianrhod, goddess of the moon.
Zodiac
These people are witty with unique personalities. Their heads are often in the clouds, and they are generous individuals who love and support the people in their lives. Strong and patient, they never complain even when life gets hard. They rely on their spiritual side to provide them with strength during adversity. Charismatic and charming, they are the life and soul of the party.

Reed Moon (October 28 – November 23)
Elements
Water and fire.
Season
Fall.
Ruling Planet
Pluto.
Color
Orange.
Gemstone
Jasper.

Animals
Owl and hound.
Ogham Letter
Ngetal (N).
Symbolism
Clarity, security, and self-expression.
Correspondences
Scorpio and Sagittarius.
Mythology
The Druids associated the reed tree with learning and wisdom. It can also bring balance to a chaotic world.
Zodiac
They never take things at face value and would dig deep until they find the truth. They are honorable, compassionate, loyal, and confident individuals, and people always love their company. Although they enjoy gossip and can get people to open up to them, these individuals are trustworthy and would never share other people's secrets with anyone.

Elder Moon (November 24 – December 23)
Element
Water.
Season
Winter.
Ruling Planet
Saturn.
Color
Gold.
Gemstone
Jet.
Animals
Raven, horse, badger.
Ogham Letter
Ruis (R).

Symbolism

Magic, death, regeneration, and rebirth.

Correspondences

Sagittarius.

Mythology

In Celtic mythology, the Elder is an enchanted tree that can protect against demons and evil spirits.

Zodiac

People born under this sign have a wild side and enjoy their freedom. They are adventurous and seek new experiences. Supportive and considerate, they help those in need. They are happy individuals who love life, and their positive attitude rubs off on their family and friends. Although they can seem superficial, they are intelligent and deep and often seek answers to life's most complicated questions.

The Celtic tree calendar still fascinates pagans and non-pagans. The use of sacred trees makes it unique and adds a mysterious side to an already interesting system. Its astrology is one of the most exciting parts of this calendar. It will allow you to learn about yourself and the people in your life from a different perspective.

Chapter 5: The Ogham Alphabet

You're probably familiar with the modern-day Roman script of the Irish language. It hasn't always been written like this. The Irish language has gone through various dialects and scripts, many of which you may be familiar with, like the traditional Gaelic format. For the most part, the modern Irish alphabet consists of 26 characters, similar to the English language, and was adapted from the scribal transcriptions of Latin texts, which is why it's somewhat legible and understandable to many people. However, did you know about the existence of another ancient writing system unique to Ireland, particularly associated with the Celts? This script has even less similarities to modern Irish than any other Celtic dialect.

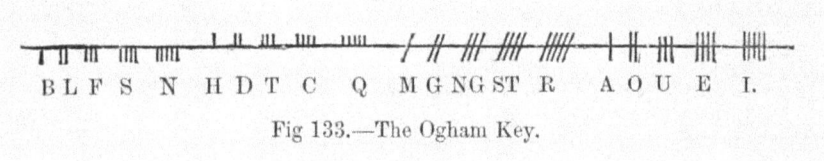

Fig 133.—The Ogham Key.

The Ogham alphabet translated to the English alphabet.[40]

This unique script is known as *Ogham*, which is pronounced as "oh-um." This language is sometimes referred to as the "Celtic Tree Alphabet" and was first discovered in Ireland approximately 1500 years ago. Although this language was initially used to communicate Primitive Irish, it was later modified and adapted for Old Irish and Walsh. Today, only a few manuscripts and inscriptions of this language have been retained, but this doesn't deter scholars from continuing to explore the meanings behind this beautiful language. This script is especially intriguing for those wanting to learn more about Celtic symbolism and also because of its visually expressive nature.

This script is considered to be ancient yet timeless. Why? Because it's still the subject of research for numerous people. The term "Ogham" is said to have been derived from the name "Ogma," which is associated with the Celtic deity known as the God of eloquence. However, the exact origins of the name are still a subject of ongoing debate. This script is also sometimes referred to as Ogam or Ogum. There is a belief held by some scholars that the term "Ogham" actually refers to the individual characters of the script, while the script as a whole is known as "Beith-luis-nin," named after the order of its letters. These letters have visuals unlike any other; each consists of a group of one to five lines arranged vertically over a baseline.

The interesting thing about this script is that it has a controversial history, with its origins still being debated by many people. The obscurity surrounding the history of the Ogham script reflects its ancient origins, as it is shrouded in the mists of time. It is widely regarded as the earliest known written script in Ireland. While some experts attribute its origin to the first century, others believe it was developed in the fourth century. Think of it like this. Ogham is so old that all of its inscriptions are on stone, and it is believed that other inscriptions could have been on sticks, stakes, and trees, which have obviously been lost with time. This chapter will provide an in-depth guide to Ogham, its history, notable features, its relation to Celtic symbolism and divination, and the meanings behind its letters.

Origin Theories

There are contradicting theories when it comes to the origins of Ogham. To be exact, four popular theories attempt to explain the development of the Ogham script. The differences in opinions arise due to the similarities between the Ogham alphabet and other scripts like Germanic runes, elder futhark, Latin, and Greek.

- The first theory proposes that the Irish created Ogham as a cryptic alphabet for political, religious, or military reasons. It was designed to ensure that those who knew only Latin would be unable to understand it.

- The second theory suggests that Ogham was invented by early Christians in Ireland as a means to develop a distinct language. This theory argues that the sounds of Primitive Irish were too difficult to transcribe into Latin, necessitating the creation of a mediating script.
- The third theory claims that Ogham was actually devised in West Wales during the 4th century. Its purpose was to merge and connect the traditional Irish language with the Latin alphabet in response to the intermarriage between the Romans and the Romanized Britons. Bilingual Ogham inscriptions featuring both Irish and Brythonic-Latin alphabets support this theory.
- The fourth theory, initially popular but later overshadowed by other explanations, posits that Ogham was invented around 600 BCE by Gaulish Druids. It was originally an oral and gestural language represented by hand signals. This theory suggests that Ogham was eventually written down in early Christian Ireland, with the lines in the script representing hand gestures or strokes. However, this theory lacks concrete evidence and remains mainly speculative.

Historical Overview

It is believed that Ogham existed as the sole writing system during the Roman Empire, from 400 to 700 AD. Back then, the most commonly used method of communication was through spoken language; even so, Ogham managed to be developed into a written version, albeit a bit late. Particularly, the Celts preferred communicating verbally; according to Julias Caesar, they used to memorize poems instead of writing them down. As a result, Ogham became the first language to be developed from spoken to written word. This script was inscribed into wood, stones, trees, and leaves during this time. Over time, the wooden inscriptions got lost, but there are several impactful stone inscriptions still present in Ireland, acting as a testament to the old language.

As the first ever written language, Ogham wasn't developed further and was only used to depict names and family trees. The stone monuments with Ogham inscriptions are thus believed to be memorials and are suggested to be hero burial grounds. Others believe that these stone monuments were boundary markers or proof of land ownership. Even though there's only evidence of Ogham in the form of stone inscriptions, many scholars believe that most inscriptions were done on leaves and trees back then. As it happens with every language or technology, the Ogham script was soon phased out when Primitive Irish was replaced by Old Irish. Afterward, the Roman alphabet was adopted and more frequently used, and Ogham's use was no more. However, some suggest that Ogham didn't disappear completely, as there were multiple guides on how to use the Ogham alphabet back in Medieval times.

Ogham inscriptions were primarily carved onto wood or stone, requiring tools like a hammer and chisel to etch messages into the material. As previously mentioned, these inscriptions often served as short memorials to individuals, earning Ogham the classification of a "memorial script." To comprehend these messages, one had to possess knowledge of the twenty characters comprising the Ogham alphabet, along with its intricacies. In the 7th century, five additional characters were introduced to the Ogham alphabet, transforming it into a usable manuscript alphabet. However, this era also marked a turning point for Ogham as it gradually faded from use due to the widespread adoption of Latin.

The investigation into the history and meanings of this enigmatic alphabet began with the discovery of the Mount Callan stone in 1785. This finding sparked the interest of archaeologists and linguists, initiating the quest to unravel the secrets of Ogham inscriptions. At first, Ogham inscriptions were mistaken for Egyptian Hieroglyphics but were later classified as different. Many connections were made with the discoveries of different stone monuments with Ogham inscriptions. The Celts were also attached to Ogham by some spectators.

Features of Ogham

Ogham is a beautiful, albeit complicated script with 25 letters grouped into five sections of five letters each. Each of these sections was named after the first letter, and the five sections total about 80 Gaelic sounds, although it's not yet decided why these sounds were grouped together in their respective sequences. It is worth mentioning that the second group is composed of stop consonants, with the exception of /h/, whereas the fourth group exclusively consists of vowels. Each letter's affiliation to a specific group can be easily determined due to its shared visual features.

The initial set of letters consists of right-sided marks, whereas the subsequent set displays left-sided marks. The third group has diagonal lines, while the fourth section features lines intersecting the central line, flowing from left to right. Interestingly, the vowels within the fourth group can alternatively be represented by dots rather than lines. Finally, the fifth group stands as the most intricate of all, with distinct symbols instead of mere linear markings. This complexity arises from the inclusion of letters introduced after 600 AD, reflecting advancements in the Irish language. Occasionally, arrowheads were utilized to indicate sentence beginnings and endings.

The Ogham Alphabet

1. B - Beith

Beith, the first letter of the Ogham alphabet.⁴¹

Beth or Beith represents the letter B in the alphabet and is linked to the birch tree. The significance of this letter is connected to fresh starts, liberation, transitions, metamorphosis, and renewal. When this symbol emerges, it serves as a reminder to let go of negativity and prioritize the positive aspects of your life.

2. L - Luis

Luis, the second letter in the Ogham alphabet.⁴²

Luis corresponds to the letter L in the alphabet and is associated with the Rowan tree. This letter symbolizes blessings, safeguarding, and gaining wisdom. The Rowan tree is renowned for its mystical protection against enchantments or magical influences. The essence of this letter encourages embracing your spiritual beliefs and maintaining a strong foundation, especially during times of uncertainty. Have faith in your own discernment and avoid being deceived by false security.

3. F – Fearn

Fearn, the third letter of the Ogham alphabet.[48]

Fearn or Fern is the equivalent of the letter F and is linked to the Alder tree. This dynamic tree represents a spirit that is continuously growing and is associated with the spring equinox. In Celtic folklore, Alder is symbolized by the courageous Bran, who acted as a bridge over a river to ensure the safety of others. Similarly, the Alder tree bridges the mystical realm between heaven and earth. When you come across this symbol, strive to be a mediator between individuals in conflict. Trust your intuition, and others will naturally seek your guidance.

4. S – Saille

Saille is associated with the Willow tree."

S or Saille is associated with the Willow tree, which is usually found near water. This letter symbolizes the knowledge and spiritual growth of a person and offers protection and healing. Saille's correspondences are that you cannot evolve without changing first and realizing that change is a part of life. So, give yourself a break, and take some time to rest spiritually.

5. N – Nion

Nion is linked to the Ash tree."

The letter N corresponds to Nion, which is linked to the Ash tree. Within Celtic heritage, the Ash tree holds sacred significance for the Druids, as it represents a connection between the inner and outer realms. This letter serves as a symbol of interconnectivity, creative energy, and transitions. When you encounter this symbol, it serves as a reminder that every action, no matter how small, carries consequences. Your choices and deeds have an impact on the future, extending beyond the present moment.

6. H – Huath

Huath symbolizes the Hawthorn trees.[46]

H symbolizes Huath, the Hawthorn tree, representing cleansing, protection, and defense. In corporal aspects, it signifies fertility, offering protection, health, and self-defense. In magical aspects, it teaches that spiritual strength can navigate thorny challenges and provide support to others.

7. D – Duir

Duir symbolizes the Celtic Oak tree.[47]

The letter D corresponds to Duir, which is associated with the Celtic Oak tree, symbolizing qualities of strength, resilience, and self-confidence. Carrying an acorn is said to bring luck in interviews and business meetings. Similar to this, it is believed that capturing a falling oak leaf will bring health in the upcoming year. The word "Duir" itself, which means "gate" or "door," conveys the significance of taking advantage of unanticipated chances and possibilities. From a magical perspective, embodying the unwavering steadfastness of the Oak empowers one to overcome spiritual challenges with unwavering strength.

8. T – Tinne

Tinne represents the Holly tree.[48]

The letter T corresponds to Tinne, which represents the Holly tree in Celtic symbolism. Immortality, harmony, bravery, and the stability of the home are all associated with the holly tree. Together, we may find strength and safety through the values of trust and honor. It is crucial to develop quick and shrewd perception when it comes to magical significance. The key to reacting to novel spiritual circumstances is flexibility and agility. Trust your instincts when it comes to maintaining a balanced strategy that balances the emotions and the mind.

9. C - Coll

Coll is associated with wisdom and creativity.[49]

The letter C, or K, stands for Coll, the Hazel tree related to knowledge, creativity, and wisdom. In August, known as the Hazel Moon, the tree bears nuts symbolizing the life force within. In Celtic mythology, hazel is associated with enchanted springs, holy wells, and divination. Whatever your creative talents are, look for inspiration. In magical aspects, allow the divine to guide your creative journey, invoking the gods for inspiration and calling upon a Muse when needing a creative spark.

10. Q - Quert

Quert represents the Apple tree.[50]

Q represents Quert, or Ceirt, which stands for the apple tree. The apple is a traditional representation of love, loyalty, and rebirth that is frequently linked to magic. In mundane aspects, making choices can be challenging. Sometimes the right decision may not bring immediate happiness, but wisdom lies in discerning what is truly needed. In magical aspects, embrace new decisions and reap the spiritual gifts they offer. Trust that valuable lessons will be learned along the way - even when things seem unclear.

11. M – Muin

Muin represents the Vine.[51]

The letter M corresponds to Muin, representing the Vine in Celtic symbolism. The Vine is associated with inward journeys and life lessons, serving as the source of grapes and wine. In terms of magical significance, it encourages engagement in prophecy and divination rituals. It is advisable to keep a record of received messages, as their meaning may become clear at a later time. When enjoying the pleasures associated with the Vine, it is important to remain mindful and avoid overindulgence, as excessive indulgence can distort one's perception of truth.

12. G – Gort

Gort represents the Ivy. [52]

The letter G corresponds to Gort, representing the Ivy in Celtic symbolism. Ivy is known for its ability to grow independently and parasitically on other plants. It thrives in diverse conditions and symbolizes the soul's journey of self-discovery across different realms. Gort is associated with growth, untamed energy, and exploring mystical aspects of personal development. Additionally, it is connected to October and the Samhain sabbat. In the physical realm, encountering Gort signifies the importance of eliminating negativity and toxic relationships from your life. In terms of magical significance, it urges you to seek internal personal growth and seek spiritual companionship externally. If you come across Gort, it might be worth considering joining or forming a group of like-minded individuals to embark on this journey together.

13. Ng – nGeatal

nGeatal represents the Reeds that grow by riversides.[53]

Ng, or nGeatal, represents the Reed that grows tall by riversides. It symbolizes direct action and purpose in one's journey. Associated with music, health, and joyful gatherings, the Reed signifies taking leadership roles, rebuilding, and making proactive decisions. In magical aspects, it highlights fruitful spiritual growth through challenges and the importance of learning valuable lessons along the path.

14. St – Straith

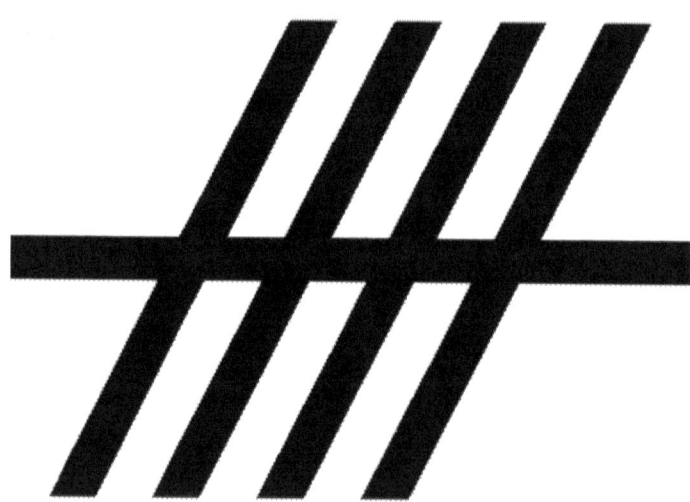

Straith corresponds to the Blackthorn tree.[54]

In Celtic iconography, the letter *St,* also spelled Straith or Straif, stands for the Blackthorn tree. Blackthorn is a symbol of power, mastery, and triumph over adversity. In everyday life, encountering Straith signifies the need to anticipate the unexpected and be prepared for changes that may disrupt your plans. It serves as a reminder that external forces can significantly impact your path. From a magical perspective, coming across this symbol indicates the beginning of a new journey where surprises, possibly challenging ones, lie ahead. Overcoming these obstacles will grant you strength and resilience. Embrace the understanding that both you and your life are undergoing transformation during this time.

15. R – Ruis

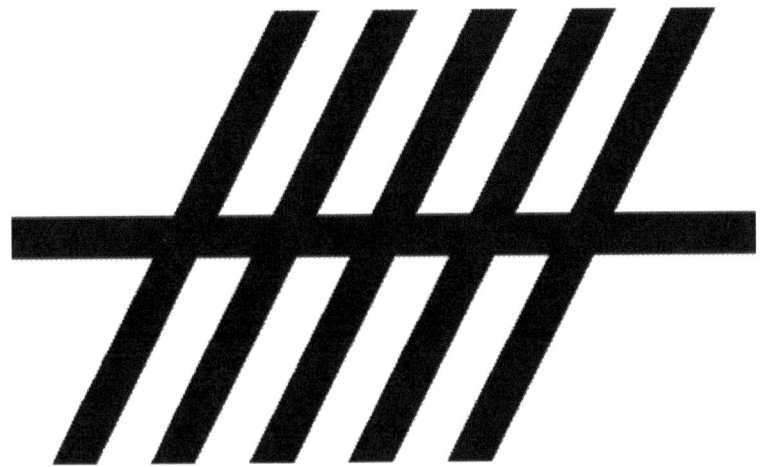

Ruis is associated with the Winter Solstice.[55]

R is the Elder tree known as Ruis, which is connected to the Winter Solstice. Elder signifies endings, maturity, and wisdom gained through experience. In daily aspects, embrace the transition between phases of life, recognizing the value of maturity and knowledge. Strive for childlike wonder while avoiding childish behavior. Magically, expect new growth stages and experiences that result in spiritual regeneration and eventual rebirth. Understand that every experience contributes to shaping the person you are destined to become.

16. A – Ailim

Ailim represents the Elm tree.[56]

The Celtic emblem for the Elm tree, Ailim, often spelled Ailm, is represented by the letter A. The Fir or Pine tree is also included in this symbol. These mighty forest giants are significant because they provide us perspective and enable us to stand above our surroundings. It signals the need to consider the bigger picture and long-term goals in real life. Be prepared for what lies ahead and embrace a broader perspective. In magical aspects, mark your spiritual growth and progress. Look to the future and envision where your newfound wisdom will lead you. Be open to guiding others who follow your path and extend a helping hand when needed.

17. – Onn

Onn symbolizes the Gorse bush.[57]

The Gorse bush, also known as Furze, is symbolized by the letter O, alternatively spelled Onn or Ohn. In life, it represents what you've been seeking is within reach, so persist in pursuing your goals. If you're unsure of your path, create a list of goals to clarify your direction and focus on the journey. In magical aspects, your spiritual journey has bestowed abundant gifts on you. Share these blessings with others and embrace leadership or mentoring opportunities that come your way.

18. U - Uhr

Ur represents the Heather plant.[58]

The Celtic emblem for the Heather plant, Uhr or Ura, is represented by the letter U. Heather represents zeal and charity. In the Celtic moors, this tough shrub lives on peat. In life, this symbol calls for destressing and seeking inner healing for the body. Listen to your physical needs and recognize the interconnectedness of physical well-being and emotional health. In magical aspects, integrate spiritual energy with physical healing. To cultivate a healthy soul, emphasize holistic healing of the body, mind, and spirit.

19. E - Eadhadh

Eadhadh symbolizes the Aspen tree.[59]

He represents the Aspen tree, which stands for fortitude and bravery, and is called Eadhadh or Eadha. When you encounter this symbol, emulate the resilience of the Aspen, staying flexible in the face of obstacles. Trust that challenges are transient, leaving you stronger. Overcome fears and reservations for personal growth. In magical aspects, resist succumbing to worldly pressures. Shift your focus to your spiritual journey, even when it feels tempting to give up.

20. I – Iodhadh

Iodhadh represents the Yew tree.[60]

The Celtic emblem for the Yew tree, Iodhadh or Idad, relates to the letter I. Because it resembles the Tarot's Death card, the Yew tree is frequently linked to concepts of death and endings. In the physical world, the appearance of Iodhadh indicates significant transitions. Embrace awareness of these changes, understanding that while not all may be negative, they will likely be substantial. Clear out unnecessary things to make room for fresh beginnings. In magical aspects, release attachment to beliefs and ideas that no longer serve you. Embrace the transformative power of change, seeing it as an opportunity rather than an obstacle. Welcome new experiences without fear and embrace the unknown.

The Ogham alphabet stands as a testament to the rich tapestry of Celtic symbolism. Its distinctive arrangement of notches and lines perfectly captures the profound connection between language, nature, and spirituality that was deeply ingrained in the Celtic culture. The Ogham script, with its roots in the ancient Celtic lands, serves as a bridge between the material and the mystical, offering a glimpse into the beliefs and wisdom of the Celts. The Ogham alphabet's association with trees and the natural world underscores the Celts' reverence for their environment. Each character corresponds to a specific tree, reflecting the interdependence between humanity and the natural realm. This intimate relationship with nature finds expression through the Ogham script, making it a unique writing system that encapsulates the Celtic worldview.

Chapter 6: The Wheel of the Year

Now that you understand the Celtic tree calendar and how it works, this chapter will focus on the ancient Irish festivals that are still popular among many Neo-pagans. These festivities celebrate nature, mark the changing of the seasons, and honor your connection with the natural world. There are eight in the Celtic wheel of the year that begins with the festival of Samhain and ends with the festival of Mabon.

The wheel of the year goes by many names: the eight Sabbats, the witches' wheel, the pagan wheel, the Irish wheel, the sacred wheel, and the Celtic wheel. It represents the seasonal cycle and festivals that the Celts celebrated at the beginning of each season. Unlike the Celtic tree system, the wheel is a solar calendar representing the cycle of plants beginning with sprouting seeds, then plants budding, blooming, and fruiting, and finally turning to seeds and repeating the cycle. Similar to the wheel, it is always turning.

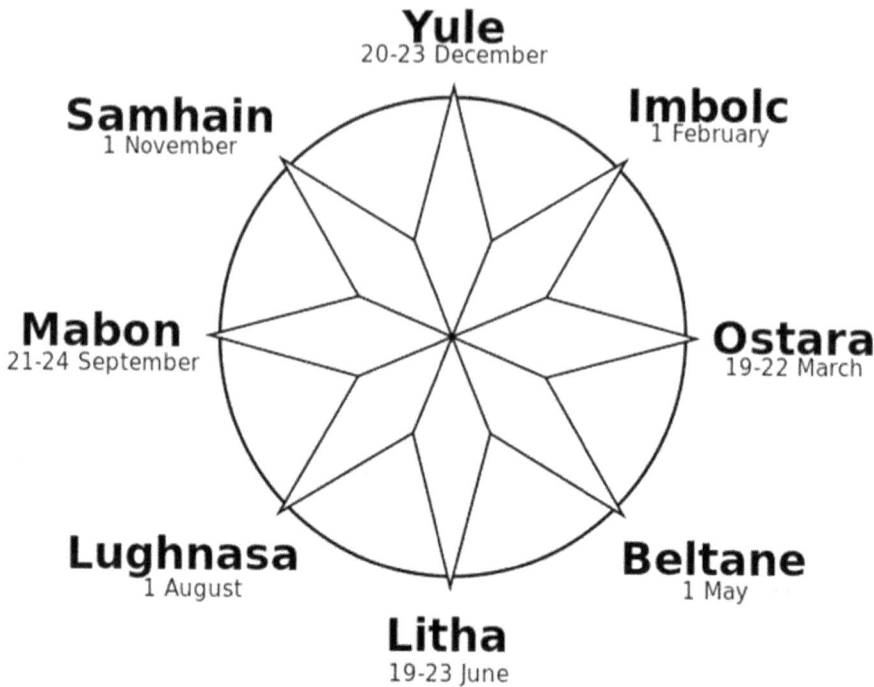

The wheel of the year.[61]

The main purpose of the wheel of the year is to connect you with nature, the cycle of the seasons, and the spirits of your ancestors, like with the festival of Samhain. It is about celebrating Mother Earth rather than honoring a specific god or goddess.

Similar to the tree calendar, the wheel of the year also represents the ongoing cycle of life: birth, death, and rebirth. However, this doesn't only apply to mankind but to nature as well. It withers and dies in the fall and winter to be reborn again in the spring and summer.

Some people think the wheel of the year is Wiccan since it celebrates and honors some pagan deities, but this isn't true. However, pagans and non-pagans can celebrate these festivals whether they worship Celtic or Wiccan deities or not.

This chapter will discuss the wheel of the year and the eight Celtic festivals, and all practices and traditions associated with them,

The Solstice and Equinox Festivals on the Wheel of the Year

The fall and spring equinoxes and the summer and winter solstice are called "The Quarter Points" and are located on the east, west, north, and south points of the wheel of the year. These points are also called "solar days" since they mark the time when the sun is at its strongest in the sky and the longest day of the year. Similarly, they can also mark the days when the sun is at its weakest in the skies and the shortest day of the year. The solstice festivals are Yule/Midwinter (December 21st) and Litha/Midsummer (June 21st).

The equinox takes place when the sun passes the equator, and the days become as long as the nights. The word "equinox" is of Latin origin. It is derived from the words "*aequus*" and "*nox*" meaning equal and night, respectively. These festivals are Ostara (March 21st) and Mabon (Sept 21st).

The cross-quarter points refer to the festivals that take place between the solstice and the equinoxes during the peak of the four seasons.

These festivals are often called the four great fire festivals or major sabbats, and they are:

- Samhain
- Imbolc
- Beltane
- Lughnasadh

Similar to zodiac signs, the quarter points on the wheel of the year are associated with the four elements.

- North is Earth
- South is fire
- East is air
- West is water

There is a fifth element at the center of the wheel called source or spirit, and it represents the invisible world that exists around you, like the soul that brings you to life and the love that unites the whole world together.

These five elements are significant in Celtic mythology and spiritual traditions. They are associated with sacred places, spirits of nature, and deities. For this reason, the ancient Celts highly revered them. Each of the eight festivals is also associated with types of crystals, colors, herbs, and plants.

The History of the Celtic Festivals

In France, historians discovered a Celtic calendar that showed the ancient Irish celebrating four fire festivals that honor the sun's movements throughout the seasons. These festivals include two equinoxes and two solstices. When the ancient Saxons and Germanic peoples intertwined with the Celts, they introduced them to the other four festivals. The eight festivals make the wheel of the year, and each one of them is celebrated every month and a half.

Although the ancient Celts and Neo-pagans celebrate these festivals to honor nature, the wheel of the year was specifically significant to the ancient Celtic farmers. They depended on it to mark seasonal changes to determine when to plow, sow, and harvest their produce.

The names of the Celtic festivals are derived from ancient cultures like the Germanic, Anglo-Saxon, Norse, and Celtic.

The Spiritual Significance of the Wheel of the Year

The wheel of the year alternates between festivals that celebrate the changes of the seasons or festivals that are inspired by ancient traditions. The Celts celebrated these occasions by providing offerings to their deities and thanking them for all their gifts. These seasonal cycles taught them that change was necessary, a significant part of nature and life to be accepted and embraced. They used this time to connect with their spiritual side and perform specific rituals to honor nature.

These festivals represent the unity between the natural and the supernatural, the spiritual and the physical world.

For many people, the solstice is a time for self-reflection since it takes place after the first half of the year. You can think about what you have achieved in the last six months and where you hope to end up by the end of the year. On the other hand, the equinox is about bringing balance to your life as you observe the equal length of the day and night and darkness and light.

The four great fire festivals allow you to enjoy life and be grateful for all the blessings nature bestows upon you each season. It is a time to connect with Mother Earth during the highest point of her seasonal cycles.

Now that you have learned about the year's wheel, the chapter's second part will focus on each of the eight seasonal festivals.

Samhain (October 31st)

Pronunciation
In Ireland, Samhain is pronounced as "Sow-wen."

Colors
Orange, gold, silver, purple, and black.

Crystals
Onyx, Bloodstone, Smokey Quartz, and Clear Quartz.

Plants and Herbs
Sage, nutmeg, garlic, rosemary, and Calendula.

Food and Drinks
Pumpkin, meat, potatoes, apples, and parsnips.

Incense
Myrrh, cinnamon, mint, frankincense, and sage.

Meaning
In Gaelic, the word "Samhain" means "end of summer." This day marks the New Year in Celtic traditions and the beginning of the wheel of the year. The Celts believed that during this time, the veil between the world of the living and the realm of the dead was at its weakest, and the spirits could roam freely between the two worlds. Although this can sound like the plot of a scary movie, for the Celts, this thought provided them with comfort. They were happy knowing the spirits of their ancestors and their departed loved ones would come and visit.

However, some of these spirits might have returned for vengeance against a person who wronged them or was responsible for their death. In this case, some people wore masks to hide from them.

It wasn't only the spirits of the dead who visited the realm of the living, but all creatures from the otherworld, such as fairies, crossed over. People protected themselves from these entities by wearing customs to hide their identities.

Practice and Rituals

Samhain rituals include feasting, dancing, building altars for the ancestors and presenting offerings, wearing masks, and carving pumpkins. Ancient Celts also had silent suppers by placing an extra seat and dish at the dining table for their dead ancestor or a departed loved one and eating in silence. They welcomed the spirits by cooking their favorite meals, leaving treats outside, and putting candles in their window to guide them.

You are correct if you feel that Samhain's rituals are quite similar to Halloween. The modern holiday is based on the ancient Celtic celebration.

Yule/Winter Solstice (December 20-23)

Pronunciation

Yule is pronounced as "Yool."

Colors

Gold, green, and red

Crystals

Clear quartz, citrine, emerald, and bloodstone.

Plants and Herbs

Oak leaves, nutmeg, cloves, cinnamon, fir, and pine.

Food and Drinks

Nuts, hot cider, wine, and soup.

Incense

Pine, cinnamon, Frankincense, and cedar.

Meaning

The festival of Yule represents rebirth, renewal, and growth. It falls on the coldest and shortest day of the year, which is referred to as the *winter solstice*. Since the Celts and Druids highly revered trees, they celebrated Yule by going outside and decorating evergreen trees, which they believed were symbols of life and survival.

Yule is also a celebration of the Oak King's victory over his brother, the Holy King. The two brothers symbolize the four seasons. King Holy ruled over Earth for the first part of the year when it was cold and dark.

However, as the days became longer, King Oak came back to life, killed his brother, and reigned over Earth.

Practice and Rituals

Many people practice Yule rituals by burning a Yule log, decorating a tree, hanging a mistletoe, making a wreath, lighting candles, preparing a feast, exchanging gifts, and building an altar. People also burned bonfires representing the sun's return since days became longer after Yule. They also celebrate this festival by singing and burning a fire where families and friends gather to throw holly to symbolize leaving the past behind and embracing the future.

The logs used in these rituals should be cut, not bought. You should also save a piece of it to burn in the next Yule as a symbol of continuity.

Christmas rituals and traditions were also borrowed from Yule.

Imbolc (February 2nd)

Pronunciation

Imbolc is pronounced as "ˈɪmbɒlk."

Colors

Light green, white, and pink.

Crystals

Bloodstone, citrine, turquoise, Amethyst.

Plants and Herbs

Witch hazel, snowdrops, cinnamon, chamomile, and blackberry.

Food and Drinks

Oats, bread, pumpkin seeds, and sunflowers.

Incense

Chamomile, jasmine, lily, and vanilla.

Meaning

Imbolc is derived from the old Irish word "*oimelc*," meaning "inside the belly" or "sheep's milk," and it represents pregnant sheep. It signifies Mother Earth's womb, where spring emerges from. This is the time of year when flowers, trees, and all other plants awaken from their long slumber.

This festival takes place between the winter solstice and the spring equinox. It represents fertility, rebirth, hope, purification, and better days.

Imbolc celebrates Brigid, the goddess of fertility, spring, poetry, and medicine. It marks the end of the cold and dark winter and welcomes spring and the agricultural season. Imbolc is a time for new beginnings and growth.

Practice and Rituals

People celebrate by lighting bonfires for purification and to honor the sun. They also make Brigid dolls or crosses from corn stalks and hang them on their doors or inside their homes. People also placed a broom at their front door to symbolize sweeping out the past and all the things that no longer serve them to make space for the future and all it has to offer.

Ostara/Spring Equinox (March 20-23)

Pronunciation

Osatra is pronounced as "oh s t aa er."

Colors

Shades of green, pink, yellow, and white.

Crystals

Rose quartz, amethyst, and aquamarine.

Plans and herbs

Snowdrops, tulips, crocus, daffodils, catnip, spearmint, lemongrass, clover, and meadowsweet.

Food and Drinks

Honey, bread, lettuce, spinach, kale, and eggs.

Incense

Narcissus, violet, jasmine, sandalwood, strawberry, and rose.

Meaning

Ostara is derived from "Eostre," the goddess of dawn and spring, and it celebrates the arrival of spring and new beginnings. In Celtic mythology, Eostre awoke from her long slumber on Ostara and resurfaced from under the ground. In another myth, the festival honors the day the goddess became pregnant with the god of the sun, who was born on Yule. Some traditions combine the two myths together.

Ostara is associated with rebirth, new life, fertility, and balance since day and night, light and dark, are equal. This is a time that gives people hope as they witness the arrival of spring after the dark and cold winter.

Practice and Rituals

People celebrate this festival by throwing feasts, lighting fires, coloring, and decorating eggs. This festival is associated with Easter, which is why they both have similar rituals and practices.

Beltane (May 1st)

Pronunciation

Beltane is pronounced as "beltayn."

Colors

Yellow, green, blue, and red.

Crystals

Rose quartz, malachite, beryl, sunstone, emerald.

Plants and Herbs

Rose, oak, primrose, paprika, meadowsweet, dandelion, hawthorne, and daffodil.

Food and Drinks

Cakes, oats, elderflower, sweet bread, and wine.

Incense

Vanilla, peach, ylang-ylang, frankincense, and rose.

Meaning

This festival marks the beginning of summer, celebrating fertility and light. The word Beltane means "Bel's fire," Bel means bright fire, and it is also the name of the Celtic god of the sun. This is the time when the day becomes longer than the night and all-natural and supernatural beings like spirits and fairies awaken from their slumber. With its burning hot fire, Beltane is associated with passion and lust.

Practices and Rituals

People celebrate Beltane by building a fairy altar, making a flower crown, praying, maypole dancing, and holding weddings. They also burn bonfires, symbolizing passion, letting go of your inhibitions, and following your heart's desire. The ancient Celts also celebrated Beltane by dancing in nature around trees. They would also dress a young girl in colorful clothes and place a wreath of flowers over her head to symbolize the goddess of spring.

The ancient Celts placed a brown branch in their homes to protect them against the fairies or other supernatural entities that awoke. Many people also get married on this day since it is associated with passion.

Litha/Summer Solstice (June 20th-23rd)

Pronunciation
Litha is pronounced just like it's written, and the "th" are soft.

Colors
Orange, yellow, gold, and red.

Crystals
Emerald, yellow topaz, calcite, citrine, and sunstone.

Plants and Herbs
Verbena, thyme, rosemary, mint, chamomile, calendula, mugwort, mullein, lavender, sage, rose, sunflower, and dandelions.

Food and Drinks
Honey, carrots, squash, ice cream, and apple cider.

Incense
Sage, lemon, orange, musk, lavender, and rose.

Meaning
Litha marks the longest day of the year when the sun is at its peak. It is also when the sun's heat begins to weaken, and the day becomes shorter. This festival takes place in the middle of the summer when nature is at its strongest, the days are warm, and the plants are flourishing.

In Celtic mythology, the Oak King gave up his kingdom to his brother, the Holy King, during Litha. It is a special occasion that honors the victory of light over darkness. It is also a symbol that no matter how dark or hard life gets, things will always get better, and the sun will shine again.

The word "*Litha*" is of Anglo-Saxon origin and means June.

Practices and Rituals
This festival is celebrated by burning bonfires, feasting, eating fresh fruits, and dancing. Ancient Celts practiced certain rituals to protect themselves against the supernatural creatures who re-emerged during Beltane since they became very powerful on Litha and could spread chaos and cause harm.

Lughnasadh (August 1st)

Pronunciation
Lughnasadh is pronounced as "LOO-nuss-uh."

Colors
Yellow, light brown, gold, and green.

Crystals
Peridot, tiger's eye, amber, golden topaz, citrine.

Plants and Herbs
Ivy, clover, blackthorn, basil, Heather, and grains.

Incense
Frankincense, rose, mint, and sandalwood.

Meaning
Lughnasadh celebrates the harvest season and marks the period between summer and fall. It is named after Lugh, the god of light and the sun, because of a legend that links him to this festival.

Lugh's mother, Tailtiu, the goddess of Sovereignty, cared more about mankind and their wellbeing than herself. She spent her days preparing the lands for cultivation. However, she worked so hard that her body couldn't take it anymore and died. Every year, Lugh would honor his mother with a lavish feast which came to be known as Lughnasadh.

This festival takes place in the last few months of the year, so it's an opportunity to reap the benefits of all your hard work. It is time for self-reflection and asking yourself if you have achieved all your goals or if you should assess your choices and decisions and make adjustments.

Practices and Rituals
The ancient Celts would present offerings from their harvest to their gods and goddesses on Lughnasadh. They would also honor Tailtiu by playing sports like boxing and wrestling. People also celebrated by lighting bonfires and getting married.

Mabon/Autumn Equinox (September 20th-23rd)

Pronunciation
Mabon is pronounced as "maybn."

Colors

Orange, yellow, gold, and brown.

Crystals

Lapis lazuli, sapphire, quartz, amber, and citrine.

Plants and Herbs

Marigold, chamomile, rosemary, and sage.

Incense

Frankincense, apple, cinnamon, pine, and sage.

Meaning

Mabon is the last festival on the wheel of the year. It is a time to reflect on your losses and gains. Although celebrating the autumn equinox is an ancient tradition, the name *Mabon* is relatively new. Wiccan writer Aidan Kelly came up with it. He named the festival after Mabon and Modron, the Welsh hunter god.

The festival marks the loss of the Celtic fertility god Cernnunos who went to the underworld every year during the autumn equinox and re-emerged as the green man to symbolize rebirth and growth,

Practices and Rituals

People celebrated Mabon by setting up an altar to honor Cernunnos and expressing their gratitude for their harvest and all the blessings nature bestowed upon them.

Each festival on the wheel of the year has its own unique name and rituals. However, there is one thing they all share in common – nature. Most people take nature and the changing of the seasons for granted, but can you imagine what the world would be like if there was only one season?

Change is necessary, and each season is a reminder that nothing in life lasts. It is a comforting thought knowing that light will always come after darkness. However, it also reminds you that sunny and warm days won't last forever, so cherish them and enjoy them for as long as they last.

Remember, the wheel of the year will always keep turning, and good days will come sooner or later.

Chapter 7: The Tree of Life

Have you ever seen an Irish person wearing a tree pendant? You probably thought it was a random piece of jewelry, but what you may not know is that this is no ordinary tree. It is The Tree of Life, one of the most significant symbols in Celtic mythology. It represents the essence of life, a popular concept that has appeared in many mythologies, religions, and cultures throughout history. The concept of the tree of life exists in different beliefs and faiths.

The Celtic tree of life.[62]

Although many ancient cultures used this symbol, it held a special meaning among the Celts, who, in turn, influenced their Irish descendants. Even though it's hundreds of years old, people still cherish it and use it in jewelry, painting, decorations, etc.

The Celts and the Druids highly revered trees. They appeared in different parts of their mythology, like the Celtic tree calendar. Trees also played a huge role in their daily lives. They were a source of food, medicine, and shelter, and they burned their wood to keep them warm during the winter. It is no wonder that the Druids considered them to be sacred. Trees have always been a source of life, and the ancient Irish depended on them in all aspects of their lives.

In Celtic mythology, trees had a spiritual significance; they acted as portals between the world of the living and the spiritual realm. The Druids also believed that the spirits of their ancestors lingered in trees which made them enchanted. Hence, they turned to their sacred trees during tough times or whenever they needed assistance. The Druids also presented offerings to the gods and chose their chiefs under trees.

The ancient Celts associated the tree of life with the forces of nature as they come together to create balance and harmony for mankind and the universe. It also represented strength, knowledge, power, wisdom, and protection. It encompassed all the natural and spiritual elements necessary for life on Earth.

The Tree of Life is a complex and multi-layered symbol that reflects ancient Irish culture and traditions. It represents stability, strength, and faith, and the Druids and Celts believed it to be the center of the universe.

This chapter will detail the significance of the Tree of Life, its different parts, and what each one symbolizes.

The History of the Tree of Life

It isn't an exaggeration to say that this symbol is as old as human beings. In Norse Mythology, the Vikings brought their Tree of Life with them when they came to Ireland, which could have influenced the Celts to create their own. It is believed that the ancient Egyptians were the first people to create and use this symbol. It was found carved on their tombs and other monuments as well. In other words, the Celts weren't the ones who invented the concept of the Tree of Life since it existed centuries before the ancient Irish civilization came to be.

While all countries and faiths consider the Tree of Life to be sacred, each assigned a different meaning to it based on their own beliefs and ideologies.

The Tree of Life in Greek and Roman Mythology

In Greek and Roman mythology, the Tree of Life is quite similar to the Celtic tree as its roots reach out to the underworld, and its branches reach to the stars or the heavens.

The Tree of Life in Ancient Egypt

The ancient Egyptians believed that the branches of the Tree of Life represented abundance and the heavens, while its roots symbolized death. In ancient Egyptian Mythology, Isis, the goddess of magic and wisdom, and Osiris, the god of death and rebirth, sprung from the Tree of Life.

The Tree of Life in Norse Mythology

The Tree of Life is also called Yggdrasil or the Viking Tree of Life. It is an ash tree and one of the most sacred symbols in Norse mythology. The Nine Worlds of the universe stood on its branches. If anything happened to this tree, the world would perish.

The Tree of Life in China

There is a famous story in Chinese mythology about an enchanted peach tree that grows fruits once every three thousand years. Whoever eats one of its fruits will be immortal. This Chinese Tree of Life is depicted differently from its Celtic counterpart. It has a phoenix at the top and a dragon at the bottom.

The Tree of Life in Mayan Civilization

The Mayans believed that when the universe was created, there was a large tree that connected the otherworld, the physical world, and heaven together. Everything in life came from this tree. This is the Tree of Life and the origin of the universe.

The Tree of Life in Buddhism

The Buddhists believe Buddha attained enlightenment while sitting under the Tree of Life, Bodhi. In Buddhism, this sacred tree represents existence and enlightenment.

Hinduism

Hindus believe their Tree of Life grows upside down; its branches are underground while its roots reach the sky. This tree blesses people and provides them with what they need to survive.

The Tree of Life in African Culture

In Africa, the Tree of Life is the Baobab tree. Although the climate in this area is dry and some plants struggle to grow, there is always fruit growing on this sacred tree. For this reason, the African people highly revere it since it is the source of nourishment and life.

The Tree of Life In Bahrain

Interestingly, in Bahrain, there is a tree in the middle of the desert standing tall in the hot and dry weather. It is over four hundred years old, and no one knows how it survived all these years since there isn't any water source close to it. It is a miraculous tree that represents power and magic. The locals refer to it as the Tree of Life.

The Tree of Life in Christianity

The Bible mentions the story of Adam and Eve and how they disobeyed God and ate from the forbidden tree. It is believed to be the Tree of Life, symbolizing God's love and wisdom.

The Tree of Life in Islam

The Forbidden Tree or Tree of Immortality is also mentioned in the Quran. Other trees in Islam resemble the Tree of Life: The Tree of Knowledge, The Infernal Tree, and The Lote Tree.

The Tree of Life in Kabbalah

In Kabbalah, a mystic branch of Judaism, the Tree of Life is a symbol or illustration, not a real tree. It connects mankind with the angel and the Divine.

The Tree of Life in Native America

Similar to the Celts, the Native Americans have many myths and legends about their sacred trees and assign a meaning to each one of them. In one of these stories, they talked about a giant tree that connected the spirit realm, the physical world, and the heavens together. This is the Tree of Life.

The Tree of Life in Celtic Mythology

The Celts and the Druids believed that trees connected them to their families, dead ancestors, and their gods and goddesses. They believed that the Tree of Life was a symbol of the afterlife and connected them to the world of the spirits and the heavens.

Myth about the Tree of Life

The Tree of Life is featured in many Irish myths and legends, but there is one tale that reflects the significance of the tree; it is the myth of the founding of Ireland.

There was a giant called Treochair who lived in the Otherworld. He brought a branch from the Tree of Life to Earth one day. He shook it a couple of times, and acorns, apples, and nuts fell from it. He then planted them in the north, south, east, west, and center of the Emerald Isle. Hence, the five sacred trees that protect and guard Ireland were created from the Tree of Life.

It's an Oak Tree

The Celts often described the Tree of Life as an oak tree since it is one of the world's most ancient, majestic, and powerful trees. If you observe any oak tree, you will notice that it is huge and one of the tallest trees you will ever see. Hence, they attract lightning. When the Celts observed this phenomenon, they believed it was a divine message from the gods commanding them to worship these trees.

"*Daur*" is the Gaelic word for "Oak," which the English word door originates from. This stemmed from the belief that the sacred trees are gateways to another world. In fact, the Celts believed that if they slept under an oak tree, they might wake up in the realm of spirits.

The Celts associated the heart of an oak tree with fertility. They also believed that inside each oak tree lies the secrets and wisdom of the universe.

Since the Druids' name is derived from the Gaelic word for oak, they were considered the guardians of the gateway to the otherworld and experts in tree magic.

Crann Bethadh

Like the Norse, the Celts had a term for the Tree of Life, called "Crann Bethadh" in Gaelic, meaning "The feeding tree." Whenever they moved to a new town or built new settlements, the first thing the Celt did was plant an oak tree to guarantee abundance and prosperity and honor the Tree of Life.

All oak trees in ancient Ireland represented this sacred symbol. It was not thought of to build a town without this majestic tree standing tall and protecting the lands. During wartime, soldiers would cut down their enemies' Crann Bethadh. They believed this would weaken their defenses and make them vulnerable and easy to defeat. In fact, they would often celebrate when they cut down their adversaries' Tree of Life because they knew their enemies would lose the war without its support.

The Main Parts of the Tree of Life

If you look at an illustration of the Tree of Life, you will notice that the branches and roots are long and in perfect symmetry, with both mirroring one another to reflect balance and harmony. This depiction isn't random. It holds a deeper meaning behind it. The long branches that reach up to the sky and the roots that stretch deep under the ground symbolize the connection between the mind and the body, the spiritual and the physical, and heaven and Earth.

The Celts were impressed by the Tree of Life's strong root system. They would observe the size and weight of the oak tree and wonder how its roots managed to carry and support something that huge. As a result, the Tree of Life became a symbol of strength. To this day, people look at it in awe of its power. Although many other Celtic symbols reflect strength, none matches the majesty of the Tree of Life.

Many ancient Irish symbols include the Celtic knot, a looped knot pattern with no beginning or end. In other words, it is infinite, which represents eternal life. The knot on the Tree of Life signifies this never-ending life cycle.

Although there are many designs of the Tree of Life, it is always shown as a tree with multiple roots and branches spread above.

Interpretations of the Main Parts of the Tree of Life

- **Roots:** The roots symbolize the connection to the earth and physical existence. They represent the foundation of life and the significance of staying grounded in one's origins. The roots also symbolize the connection to the past and the wisdom of the elderly. They also represent the origin of one's family, like the ancestors or grandparents.
- **Trunk:** The trunk symbolizes the body and physical strength. It represents the ability to stand tall and weather the storms of life. It also symbolizes the connection between the spiritual world and the material world. It also represents the parents as they act as a

link between the roots and the leaves. The trunk of the tree exists on Earth.
- **Branches:** The branches represent growth and expansion. They symbolize the potential for personal and spiritual growth and the ability to reach the heavens. The branches also represent the eternal life of the human soul.
- **Leaves:** The leaves symbolize abundance, fertility, and renewal, as well as the cycles of life and death that are part of the natural world. They also represent the offspring of a family.

The Tree of Life Symbolism

There are various interpretations of this ancient Celtic symbol. Since there aren't many records about the Celts or how they used to live their lives, scholars researched and analyzed the little information they have to develop these explanations. Since nothing is concrete, you can come up with your own interpretations. The tree can mean something different to many people depending on how it makes you feel.

The meaning behind the Tree of Life has also changed since the time of the Celts. However, one interpretation remains the same – that it represents the circle of life.

Immortality

The oak tree is one of the longest-living trees in the world, as it can live for six hundred or even one thousand years. When the tree roots and begins to die, its acorn seeds can grow into a large oak tree. Interestingly, this is the perfect representation of the circle of life. This also led the Celts to believe that the oak tree was immortal, while others believed it was their reincarnated ancestors.

Spiritual Connection

The circles found in many illustrations on the Tree of Life symbolize inclusion and connection. The tree also represents the connection between the physical and spiritual realms, the bridge between heaven and Earth. This shows that all living beings in the heavens and on Earth are linked together through the Tree of Life.

Rebirth and Change

One can tell the seasons are changing by observing the trees. In the fall, their leaves turn yellow; in the spring, their flowers bloom, and the leaves are full of life. However, the trees don't wither and die when the weather changes. They remain strong and adapt to change and keep growing.

The leaves falling in winter and growing in spring represent rebirth and human life. Even though you experience changes all the time, whether negative or positive, you keep growing and learn to endure and embrace whatever life has to offer.

Wisdom and Strength

Wisdom has always been associated with old age. Hence, oak trees became a symbol of wisdom and strength among the Celts. They watched this tree standing tall for centuries against thunder, rain, storms, and constant attacks from animals and human beings.

The Celts believed that since the oak trees spent more time on Earth than any other human, they had seen many things in this world and endured adversities by being exposed to tough weather conditions. They became a symbol of knowledge and endurance.

Family

The Tree of Life doesn't only symbolize the link between heaven and Earth but also family connections. There is a reason people often use the term family tree when they talk about their ancestors. The branches represent old family members and all the children who have been born.

If you look at your family tree, you will see pictures of your departed ancestors and your family's new members. This symbolizes the circle of life, with one life ending and another beginning.

Growth

Since trees live for centuries, they grow slowly throughout hundreds of years. The oak tree began its life as a small seed that grew over time into a large tree. The Tree of Life can represent growth and how human beings keep growing and changing until the end of their lives.

Rituals and Celebrations

Trees played a big role in the Druids' rituals and Celtic festivals and celebrations. For instance, to celebrate Beltane, the Celts would decorate a tree with flowers and ribbons to symbolize the Crann Bethadh and dance around it. During Samhain, they would gather around oak trees and pray to their ancestors.

The Tree of Life in Modern Times

Many Irish people still hold on to their ancestors' beliefs. If you visit Ireland, you will see how they incorporate ancient symbols in many designs. The Tree of Life will always be popular and special among Irish people of all ages. Some even get it tattooed on their body.

It is also one of the most common designs engraved on Irish urns since it shows that death isn't the end. It is a reminder that your loved ones aren't gone forever; they will be reborn. On the surface, the Crann Bethadh looks like a regular tree, but when you learn its true meaning, it can provide comfort. Death isn't something to be feared but merely a chapter in one's ongoing cycle of life. In some ancient cultures, funerals were happy events because they knew that the person would either be reincarnated or spend eternity in the otherworld.

Many cultures and religions believed in the Tree of Life before the Celts. It was a popular concept for which many people assigned meaning, legend, and beliefs. They believed that the Tree of Life was powerful and held the universe together and that the world would cease to exist without it.

All ancient cultures needed the concept of the Tree of Life. They wanted something bigger than them to represent the cycle of life and remind them that death wasn't the end. The Celts created this symbol to connect them to all the things that were out of their reach, like the heavens, the spirit realm, and their departed ancestors. The Tree of Life provided them with comfort that the universe was safe and in good hands.

The Celts and the Druids held trees in very high regard. When reading about their history, you will find that they played a big role in their daily lives, religious practices, and spirituality.

Looking around in nature, you will find that nothing is more powerful or majestic than trees. They manage to stand tall and remain strong no matter what the forces of nature throw at them. The Celts found them inspiring. If you spend some time in nature too and reflect on these magnificent plants, you will be moved by them as well.

Chapter 8: Animals as Celtic Symbols

Animals influenced numerous parts of ancient Celtic life. They shaped their religion, society, warfare, economics, art, and literature. This chapter delves into the role that animals played in Celtic mythology and spirituality. By reading it, you'll understand what animism is and its significance in ancient Celtic society. You'll find out how the ancient Celts approached and interacted with animals and come across plenty of interesting and informative tales of animal-related deities in the Celtic pantheon.

Animists are able to connect with nature spiritually and mystically.[63]

What Is Animism?

There's a common misconception that animism is a religion. While animism is deeply tied to the world of spirituality, it is a culture-specific outlook on the universe. Animists believe that there is another world where spirits reside. According to this belief, spirits can meddle with human affairs, offer protection and guidance, or harm people. Animism is the belief that everything in nature, such as plants, animals, rocks, and bodies of water, has a spirit.

Animists have a unique way of experiencing the world. They know how to connect with nature by understanding the energetic frequencies that connect everything. Since animists have higher energetic vibrations and are tuned into the universe's energies, they have higher levels of consciousness. This enriches their spiritual endeavors and makes them more responsive to the natural and spiritual worlds. Animists understand that the otherworldly is interconnected with the terrestrial.

Ancient Celts and Animism

Animism was interwoven into the ancient Celtic tradition because, at the time, the world was predominantly based on nature and all things natural. Wild animals roamed freely, and humans developed a forest culture. They prayed to the oak trees, lived in mountains and forests, sought shade beneath the trees, and hunted and gathered for sustenance. They thrived on agriculture and based their calendar and festivities on the sun and agronomy. It goes without saying that the ancient Celts were a lot more connected to nature than the humans of the modern-day world.

The ancient Celts relied on natural resources to survive, which is why they prayed fervently to their gods for abundant harvests, fertile soil, and good weather. They believed they must give back to the world and the deities to reap the rewards of Earth, which is why they lived harmoniously and deeply connected to nature. They performed rituals, made offerings, and lived conscientiously to play their part in the universe.

Ancient Celts believed everything in nature was protected by a spirit guardian. They also thought that animals were the messengers of the deities. Some accounts suggest that ancient Celts believed that some of the deities manifested in the form of animals, while others claim that they revered nature without necessarily thinking that the deities took the form of animals. Regardless of the relationship between animals and deities, springs, hills, caves, and rivers, along with other elements of nature, were considered sacred.

The Celts held rituals and prayers in certain locations in nature because they believed they served as a portal to the spiritual realm. They set up shrines and places of worship close to groves of trees. This is where they held their social and spiritual meetings and called on the magical powers of the oaks for help and advice. The ancient Celts had secret groves of trees that they called the *nemeta*. They believed that these represented the unity between the earth and the heavens. The roots symbolized the Earth, and the branches embodied the sky.

Ancient Celts also believed celestial bodies, the weather, and other phenomena like storms and tsunamis were living beings. To ensure that the sun continues to shine, rain pours at adequate levels, and the sea stays neither too calm nor too angry, they had to appease and acknowledge these entities. The Celts were particularly concerned with thunder, seen in the many depictions of this phenomenon. To underscore the significance of thunder, the Celts worshipped Taranis, who was not only the god of thunder but was the personification of the occurrence itself.

What They Learned from Animals

The Celts believed they had a lot to learn from animals. Even though animals have their own languages, brains, and psyches, they are still intertwined with nature. Animals are fully present and aware of their surroundings when they are in nature. Animists closely interpret animal behavior and believe they can receive messages from the universe or higher powers through them or see omens in changes in their behaviors. Deities that share similar characteristics with certain animals were often named after them. *Epona*, the goddess of fertility and the protector of the equine, means "horse," and the Celtic bear goddess' name, Artio, also means "bear."

Ancient Celts found at least a few traits to admire about nearly every animal. They were certain that animals were blessed with a unique presence that humans could never fulfill, as well as traits and abilities that humans lacked. They knew the only ethical way to benefit and learn from these abilities was to honor animals and approach them with humility and respect.

Animals in Celtic Mythology

The Tale of the Cailleach

One Scottish Celtic myth revolved around a storm hag. Cailleach, the hag, embodied the force of nature and was responsible for triggering the first snowfall of the season. The crone was usually illustrated wearing a drab, enormous plaid cloak. She had a ghastly blue face and long, white hair. Being the hag deity of winter, Cailleach's hair carried speckles of frost.

The Celts believed she had one eye in the middle of her forehead, signifying her ability to see everything that happens in all the realms. This was a characteristic shared by all omnipresent deities.

The Gaelic term "*Cailleach*" is derived from the word "pallium" in Latin, which translates to "veil." The ancient Celts may have chosen the name "veiled one" to refer to the crone deity to highlight her mysterious essence. Cailleach, however, is now loosely interpreted as the "old wife."

Legend says Cailleach went to a strait near the coast to wash her plaid. The tartan cloak was too huge and heavy that it stirred up a raging storm. The Gulf of Corryvreckan, the strait she was at, is known today for being one of the largest whirlpools on Earth. The term "*Corryvreckan*" translates to "cauldron of the plaid."

The crone's cloak became as white as snow and draped over the entire country during winter. Celtic animists believe Cailleach is the Scottish pantheon's most powerful deity. At the time, the winter was so long and harsh that people had to approach and acknowledge it courteously. Deities in other parts of the world, like Greece, were known for their beauty and what were regarded as ideal features at the time. This is why many people don't understand why anyone would worship a crone.

With little technology and nowhere to hide from the scorching heat of summer, freezing winters, wild animals, and other natural phenomena, ancient Celts understood that nature was unexpected, unsparing, and terrifying. Cailleach embodied this obscure, scary aspect of nature and was highly venerated for it.

Robert I and the Spider

The king of Scotland at the time, Robert I, fled to the Western Isles of Scotland after his army was conquered in war. He found a secluded cave in the isles, where he sought refuge and carefully curated a plan. Spending at least a few months there, the king often occupied himself by watching a spider as it meticulously built its web.

After Robert I, the king of Scotland, was defeated in battle, he sought refuge in the Western Isles of the nation. He ended up staying in a cave for a few months as he planned his next step. According to legend, the king watched a spider painstakingly build a web. Even though the average spider takes around 60 minutes to construct its shelter, the weather made the process particularly difficult for this arachnid.

Storms took the web apart each time the spider created it. The little creature, however, didn't give up. It kept rebuilding the web until it finally succeeded. Having been raised in an animist society, Robert I learned a lot from the spider. The message was clear: he needed to tackle what was in front of him without giving up, and this message needed to be spread to everyone.

Animism and Hunting

Even though ancient Celts revered animals, they still had to hunt for sustenance. They still approached their prey with honor and respect because they believed their lives depended on these animals' lives and deaths. They believed hunting was a venerated activity, and they couldn't take the lives of the hunted without the blessing of the corresponding deities. They sometimes sacrificed domestic animals to the corresponding deities to earn their blessings.

They also believed that they weren't harming nature by killing animals. Even though they took something from nature, they gave it something in return. The bloodshed from dead animals was thought to contain necessary nutrients and revitalizing power. The sacred act of hunting was celebrated because it contributed to the growth of nature, the lives of hunters, and the people they fed.

The Legend of the Selkie

Ancient Celts believed that some spirits came from several worlds at once. The selkie, a mythological creature, was one of them. Scottish selkies were thought to be powerful enough to transform from their seal-like form into a human once they left the sea. There is a tale of a man who spotted a selkie while he was on the beach.

This selkie took the form of a beautiful woman. The man fell in love and decided to steal the seal skin she'd shed so she could stay human. He forced her to marry him and carry his children. She spent most of her time gazing at the sea, missing what had been her home. A few years later, the woman finally found her selkie skin and jumped into the ocean. She loved her children but still wanted to go home. Some versions of the tale recount that the selkie visits them every year.

The Cunning Kelpies

The Kelpie is another shapeshifting creature in Scottish mythology. The horse-like figure can take human form, but some accounts suggest that it keeps its hooves. Some researchers explain that the Christian beliefs surrounding Satan and hooves come from this. Kelpies are believed to inhibit the isolated rivers and areas of Scotland. Kelpies are mainly white or grey and have long, wet manes. They appear to their victims, somehow convincing them to get on. Once the human rides the kelpie, the pony takes off and drowns them in the water.

The Morrigan and Cu Chulainn

The Morrigan, the deity of war, is popularly known as the Triple Goddess. The deity could tell which warriors would die in battle before it was time to fight. Her predictions also allowed her to steer the war's outcome in her desired direction. She was able to shapeshift into a crow and flew over battlegrounds. Crows are generally believed to be a bad omen, which is why her presence either struck fear into the nerves of warriors or motivated them to fight harder.

The goddess fell in love with Cu Chulainn, a heroic warrior who was half human and half divine. Known for her beauty, the Morrigan could seduce the most powerful of men. However, her tricks didn't work on Cu Chulainn when she approached him before he went to war. He turned her down, which drove her to seek revenge.

Mid-battle, the goddess decided to shapeshift into an eel, swim up to the warrior hero, and trip him. Cu Chulainn naturally punched the animal away and continued to fight. The deity once again transformed into a gigantic wolf. She ran at him, pushing cattle toward the hero. Once again, he fought back and threw a stone into the wolf's eye. The Morrigan went temporarily blind but shifted into a cow for one last time. She gathered a herd of cows and moved toward Cu Chulainn.

He, however, quickly moved out of the herd's way and threw another stone at the Morrigan. This time, the stone hit and broke her leg. Hurt enough, the goddess decided to accept defeat. After the warrior hero won the battle, he met an old woman on his way back to the base. The lady was milking a cow, but Cu Chulainn was too tired to notice her leg and eye injuries. Not recognizing that she was the Morrigan, he stopped right in front of the woman and sparked a conversation with her.

The woman, who appeared gentle and harmless, offered Cu Chulainn a glass of milk which he accepted. He downed the entire glass, but little did he know that drinking the milk would heal the Morrigan and give her strength. The Morrigan didn't care to fight Cu Chulainn anymore. Tricking him into healing her was revenge enough for her.

The warrior hero and the goddess crossed paths once again right before he died. Cu Chulainn was heading to another battle when he saw a woman scrubbing blood off the armor. He knew that this sight was a very bad omen when he was about to face an enemy. Cu Chulainn continued walking toward the battlefield regardless.

This battle, just as he anticipated, was the end of Cu Chulainn. He was severely wounded but still managed to fight until his last breath. The hero tied himself to a boulder, hoping to scare any enemies passing by. The Morrigan, in the form of a cross, rested on his shoulder until he passed away peacefully.

Cernunnos the Antlered God

Cernunnos was a deity who appeared in half human half stag form. He was brought into the world during the winter solstice, known as the year's darkest day. Even though he was associated with the harsh, dreary winter, the deity married Beltane, the goddess of spring. However, their happiness wasn't long-lasting because he died six months later on the summer solstice. The Celts believed him to be a wise teacher, which is why they depicted him cross-legged.

Cernunnos was the deity of the underworld, animals, prosperity, and fertility. Very little about the antlered god is known, further reinforcing his mysterious facade. No mythological tales emerged about him, so most of what is known about him is from Celtic iconography. His most notable depiction shows him carrying a serpent and a torc, surrounded by a number of animals – like a raven, dog, and stag. Cernunnos ruled over nature and animals. Researchers suggest that ancient Celts brought the deity offerings of elk, snakes, wolves, and other animals to thank them for creating peace between enemies. He was an esteemed protector and wise man among the tribes.

Another image portrays the deity as a bald man with the ears of a stag. His bald head is an allusion to eldership and wisdom. His antlers are thought to be a reflection of his humility and groundedness. The torque reflects his powerful status and ability to conquer enemies and offer courage and protection to those needing them.

The belief that he was born on the winter solstice and died on the summer solstice suggests that he's associated with heightened energy levels, incredible spiritual experiences, and augmentation. However, since he died just inside the second half of the agricultural cycle, the antlered god wasn't blessed with the introspective traits associated with the harvesting season. It also signifies his lack of "completeness" as a symbol of masculinity and potency. Cernunnos' marriage to Beltane, however, brought some balance into his life.

The Significance of the Stag

The stag is a symbol of wisdom and knowledge in Celtic traditions. This animal is also associated with the natural cycle of life. It symbolizes life, death, and rebirth since it regrows a new set of antlers every year. White stags are also particularly spiritually significant because they represent purity. They're related to divine energies and spiritual enlightenment.

Stags are powerful animals, which makes them symbols of masculinity, motivation, and vitality. Many spiritual individuals believe that crossing paths with a stag serves as a reminder of one's inner strength and perseverance. These are the spirit animals to turn to or animals to observe whenever you feel stuck in life.

Stags are naturally inclined to live in solitude, so animists believe they can learn how to be independent and self-reliant from them. Stags remind people that alone time is necessary to reflect and experience mental, emotional, and spiritual growth.

The stag is believed to be the protector of the other animals and is therefore seen as the king of the forest. Leadership, guardianship, and guidance are among a few of this animal's qualities, which is why deities associated with it, such as Cernunnos, take on significant roles in their society. The stag also bridges between terrestrial and heavenly matters, as well as the masculine and the physical. It brings harmony and balance into the world, which is why ancient Celts also believed it to be a spiritual messenger. Encountering a stag meant that they needed to become more spiritually involved or be more receptive to signs from the divine.

Regardless of whether you believe in Celtic mythology and folklore, you can learn a lot from the ancient Celts. Observing how animals interact with nature, treating them with respect, and understanding their role in the world can enrich your spiritual experience and heighten your consciousness. The next time you see a spider spinning its web, or a seal moving toward the shore, ask yourself how an animist or ancient Celt would have reflected on the occurrence.

Chapter 9: Celtic Divination

Divination is a method of seeking knowledge about unknown events from the future. The ancient Celts used divination to uncover what lies beneath the surface of what was happening around them and how it connected with the universe. The most widespread Celtic divination method involves the Ogham alphabet, which has become a popular prophecy tool in modern times but was not well documented in ancient times. Different techniques for Ogham divination were passed down through generations, and it's unknown which one the ancient Celts considered the most accurate. The Ogham divination method is most commonly used in Ireland, from where the Ogham letters are believed to originate.

The Celts decipher Ogham symbols to know more about their future."

The Ogham methodology works just like any other divination tool. After researching it and familiarizing themselves with the method, the practitioner gets comfortable handling it regularly. Then, they can ask questions about events, situations, people, and outcomes they're interested in. The inquiry can be made to the deities, the Spirit of Ogham, and spiritual guides with whom one wants to connect or work. You can present your question verbally or write them down and incorporate either method into your divination rituals. You can ask any question you want, but beginners are advised to keep their inquiries simple. By asking one simple question at a time, you can focus on it and the answer much better. Once you practice this for a while, you can start making more complex inquiries during divination.

Using Ogham divination is a great way to learn to understand yourself - to see how your life unfolds and understand why - and, if needed, make changes to achieve different results. In ancient times, Celts used this tool to ensure a plentiful harvest, favorable endings in battle, and similar feats. The Ogham divination is mentioned in several Irish poems, including the Bríatharogaim (Morainn mac Moín, Maic ind Óc, and Con Culainn), all of which were commonly used as divinatory insights by the Old Irish. Some modern practitioners still use these texts as poetic tools for memorizing the names of the letters of the Ogham alphabet and the spiritual meanings attached to them.

Nowadays, practitioners use Ogham to figure out how to move forward in life - by changing certain aspects of it. It's a particularly popular method among Druids, who undergo lengthy training to gain experience in deciphering complex spiritual messages they receive from deities and spirit guides. Of course, you don't have to practice it for years as they do, but you'll still need to be patient if you're a complete beginner. Without any knowledge of divination and how to interpret the messages, it will take some time to learn how to do this. You can start by choosing a part of your life you want to explore and focus on it while practicing.

Ogham divination relies on a set of 25 symbols, each associated with the letters of the ancient Irish Gaelic writings. Each Ogham symbol denotes a letter's name related to the others within its Aicme (grouping). The symbols hold the key to the layered and deep-seated meanings you can apply when interpreting the answers to your questions. Depending on the context, each letter can have a different symbolism.

According to the Neo-Pagans, and other New Age practitioners, Ogham divination hails from a version of the Celtic Tree Oracle and is based on the Celtic Tree Calendar. Older sources claim that this is inaccurate. They assert that there is much more to the Ogham than its connection to tree lore, which New Age practitioners typically focus on. The tree-based philosophy is featured in the Book White Goddess, written by Robert Graves, a prominent English poet, critic, and historical novelist. Those who base their work on ancient Celtic and Druidic traditions see tree associations as a necessary part of understanding prophetic messages but do not rely exclusively on them. They combine it with other divination methods or spiritual work.

Casting and Reading Ogham Symbols

Traditionally, the Ogham symbols are etched into wooden staves. The staves are then used during divination rituals. However, since they're just simple lines anyone can replicate, the symbols can be inscribed and even written on any surface. You can simply pen them on paper, carve them into small wooden sticks to create your own set or buy them in the most convenient form.

Ogham symbols are read from the bottom up. Traditional methods for casting the staves include drawing them from a bag, throwing them onto a cloth, or arranging them in a specific pattern.

The drawing method is typically recommended for beginners. Here is how to do it:

1. Fill a bag with your staves – you can also use a box, hat, or whatever vessel is convenient for you.
2. Pick one stave and get it out from the vessel without looking at it.
3. Focus on your intention, ask a question, and look at the symbol. Think about what it means to you. You can also consult the predefined meanings of the symbols.
4. When you feel you've received an answer, complete your reading by putting the staves away.
5. If you didn't get an answer or don't know how to interpret it, don't worry. This is common for novices and just means you have to practice.
6. Once you get the gist of the practice, you can start picking three staves out from the vessel and following the same steps shown

above. These are avenues to learn about past, present, and future outcomes.

Choosing and casting several staves by laying them out on a piece of cloth is another easy-to-do method. Here is how to execute it:

1. Choose the number of symbols you want to interpret. Depending on your experience and the nature of the information you seek, this can vary from three to six to nine.
2. Lay a piece of cloth in front of you. Do this in a quiet place where you won't be disturbed.
3. Reach into the container with the staves and start getting them out. Throw them down in front of you one by one.
4. As you take each stave into your hands, think about your intention and the questions you want to ask. Take a few moments to connect your intention with each stave.
5. Take a few additional moments to look at them when they're all in front of you and contemplate their meanings.
6. When ready, think about how the symbols you see can answer your question or queries.

Creating a spread requires more experience and is recommended for those who have mastered the first two techniques. Here is how to do it:

1. Consider what you want to learn during the reading. For example, you can explore past, present and future outcomes, spiritual, emotional, and physical aspects of your life, or your connections to a deity, ancestors, and spirits.
2. Draw three staves from your vessel and lay them out in front of you. Focus on the trio of aspects you've chosen to explore.
3. For example, if you picked the time aspects, the first stave will give your answers about past events affecting your outcome, the second one about the present, and the third about what you can expect in the future.
4. Ruminate on the meanings of the staves in front of you. When you have your answers, finish the ritual.

While the one-stave method usually relies on the upright meaning of the symbols, if you're going to use any other technique, consider the staves' reverse symbolism too. Another helpful tip is always to have an open mind when making a prophetic inquiry and waiting for an answer.

Consider various options and avoid asking questions that can be answered with a "yes" or a "no." Remember, there are no right and wrong answers either. While the explanation you get could make sense to you right away, if you keep listening to your intuition, it will soon become much clearer.

Cultivating Your Relationship with the Symbols

The best part of Ogham divination is that you can cultivate a personal relationship with the symbols and their energies. This practice relies on skills that allow you to engage with the physical, emotional, spiritual, and mental parts of yourself. Naturally, you'll need discipline and patience, but the results will be all the more rewarding. You'll unlock your natural potential, connect with your past, present, and future and reclaim balance and harmony in your life. You'll learn how you fit into this universe, reveal your purpose, and learn about your heritage (if you're interested in exploring a potential Celtic ancestry).

To build a connection with the symbols, you must also engage with two realms of Celtic cosmology, the Otherworld and the real world. This will give you access to information hidden from most people – and use this knowledge to improve your life and the life of those around you. Below are some of the best ways to cultivate your relationship with Ogham symbols.

Developing Deeper Awareness and Mindfulness through Meditation

A great way to form a connection to the symbols is by developing and enhancing your awareness and mindfulness skills. Meditation is a mindfulness technique designed to improve focus, which is the first step in gaining awareness of yourself and your surroundings. When you meditate, you start noticing a powerful sense of presence – the presence of your energies. You're opening up to the possibility of encountering and embracing new connections and relationships.

Meditation also helps you see what truly matters and focuses your energy on manifesting your intention. Most of the time, this means taking actions that will cause changes. Meditation can help you reach insights about your inner world, so you can make more informed choices.

Implementing Ogham Practices in Your Life

Regular Ogham rituals and practices are fundamental to improving your spiritual and mental health, which, in turn, will help you form stronger connections with the Spirit of Ogham and the deities and guards you choose to work with. A great way to start introducing Ogham practices into your daily life is by observing the Moon while holding the symbols.

As you do this day after day, you start feeling the changes in your energy and the energies of the signs. Patterns will emerge, and a cyclical alignment will begin. It's a good idea to keep a record of what you encounter to see how your connection with the symbols develops over time.

Besides drawing an Ogham symbol every day, you can begin doing small daily rituals like setting intentions, holding the staves in your hand as you meditate, or dedicating time to silently contemplate the staves' meanings. Consciously connecting with the symbols daily is a fantastic way to improve focus, eliminate distractions and raise your awareness. You'll feel more in tune with yourself, the symbols, and the realms in Celtic cosmology.

Opening Yourself Up to Natural Energies

To connect with the symbols, you must learn how to embrace the natural energies around you. Opening up to these energies will allow you to work with any spiritual tools, including Ogham divination. Take a few minutes daily to spend time with the staves and fully feel their energy. They can be powerful, but don't be afraid or discouraged. Invite them into your life. Do this in the open, where you can feel closer to the natural world. Just sit in a secluded spot in nature and take in everything around you - the scents, the images, the sounds, and everything you notice about your surroundings. Alternatively, you can spend time in liminal spaces where you can also be close to the Otherworld. It's critical to explore its energies too. The spirits can be great allies in a divination practice.

Interpreting Ogham Readings

Besides being a powerful divination tool, Ogham symbols represent a unique mixture of mystical and mundane wisdom, which resonate within everyone. Their meanings are deeply connected with the natural cycles of life and the traditions of the ancient Celts. Make sure you consider this when learning how to interpret Ogham readings.

Here are a few other factors to consider when interpreting the symbols:

- Each symbol is associated with a sacred tree but can have many other metaphorical meanings you can connect to spiritually.
- The vast knowledge the symbols convey guarantees that you'll take the time to slow down. You'll need time to learn their unique meanings.

- You can interpret Ogham symbols like runes and Tarot cards by assigning an intention and question to them and then choosing how to present them.
- One-stave and three-stave readings work best for beginners because they're simple enough to interpret.

Here is an example of how to do this in practice:
1. In the morning, form a question you want to be answered. For example, you can ask something like:
2. "What should I do to make the best out of this day?"
3. Focusing on the question, take three staves out of their bag or box. Lay them side by side.
4. The one on the left will provide information about yourself, the one in the middle shows events and situations you'll encounter during the day, and the one on the right shows you the outcome.
5. Look at the symbols to see their position and possible meaning. Are any of them reversed? If yes, this could indicate that something is contrary to what you would like it to be.

Working with the Symbols

There are numerous ways to work with Ogham symbols. For example, you can incorporate them into meditation or combine them with other forms of divination. If you choose the latter, you can, for instance, choose dreamwork or journeying. Dream prophecy is recommended for beginners who struggle with working out and interpreting messages while awake. To do this, you only need to take a stave (or three) and ask the question you want answered before going to sleep. The resolution will come in your dreams. Keep a piece of paper on your nightstand. You should record the messages you've obtained as soon as you wake up.

Ogham Meditation

When working with Ogham, a meditation technique that relies on the ancient Tree Lore can give much better insight. Channeling tree energy while meditating enables you to become even more familiar with the spiritual energies around you, including the ones in the symbols. Although the instructions will ask you to start your circle from the North, feel free to begin with the direction that resonates with you. Some practitioners prefer to start from the East, while others will alternate approaches depending on the seasons.

Tools you'll need:
- Wooden staves - or wands. Some practitioners prefer using trees associated with the Ogham alphabet. However, you can use the staves that symbolize them too.
- One large candle
- Incense
- A small container, preferably glass or ceramic - for the incense
- A cup of wine, beer, or mead
- Any object you want to use to improve focus
- Working surface - a portable altar or a small table you've cleared off
- A chair or cushion - depending on where you'll be sitting
- Music or sounds to meditate - optional
- Athame - optional
- Ritual clothing or jewelry, talismans - optional
- Four smaller candles represent the four cardinal directions

Instructions:
1. Choose the best place to meditate. If you're conducting the ritual outdoors, find a secluded natural environment. If you're meditating indoors, ensure that nothing and no one will disturb you.
2. Set an intention for your meditation ritual. It will help you remain focused.
3. Choose the trees with the energy you want to channel. For example, for strength and growth, you'll need oak. For balance and empathy, use holly. Whereas for protection and warding off negative energies, it's best to work with hawthorn.
4. You can use one wand or stave or different ones with similar energies to enhance a particular intention. Avoid channeling the essence of more than three trees at a time. Beginners are advised to use only one tree.
5. Arrange the four smaller candles so they're placed on the East, West, North, and South to complete a sacred circle. It will help you channel and balance the energies within the circle.

6. Set up a table or portable altar in the middle of the circle. Place the large candle, the wands or staves, the incense, and the item for focus on the table or altar.
7. Once all the items are on the table, light your incense and the candle while focusing on your intention. If you wish, start the meditation music or sound recording.
8. When you're ready to begin the ritual, take a deep breath and face North. Continuing breathing deeply, welcome the element of the Earth and the essence of the tree you're trying to channel. Think about the properties of this tree and express your respect for them silently or out loud.
9. Moving clockwise, repeat the step from above in the direction of East, South, and West, respectively. While doing this, touch the stave or wand a couple of times to empower your physical connection with the tree.
10. If you're using an athame, point it in the direction you're facing each time. Once you've greeted the tree in the last direction, you've completed your sacred circle.
11. Depending on your beliefs and practices, you can now invite and welcome any spiritual guide or deity into the circle.
12. Sit in front of your table or portable altar. Once again, you can choose which direction you want to face. Just make sure you're comfortable, so you can focus on your intention and the objects you'll use to manifest it.
13. Take a few moments to observe the candle, the staves or wands, and any other items you use for focus.
14. When you have become familiar and connected with the latter, take a sip from the cup. Feel the liquid travel through you, relaxing your mind, body, and spirit.
15. Use a familiar meditation technique for further relaxation. For example, you can choose to let your eyelids drop slowly while breathing deeply and focus on how this makes you feel. Or you can gaze into the candle while breathing deeply – until you relax and reach a deeper stage of consciousness.
16. Once you're in a deep meditation state, you'll be ready to explore the realms of wisdom, divination, and inspiration. Remain in this state for as long as you desire.

17. When your meditation is complete, you'll need to close the ritual. Begin by facing West, thank the element of water and the tree energy for their assistance, and bid them farewell.
18. If you've summoned any spiritual guides or deities, send a quick prayer of gratitude to them as well.
19. Move anti-clockwise towards the South, East, and North. Once again, the direction to start with is optional, but make sure to move anti-clockwise from whichever direction you begin dismantling the ritual.
20. Extinguish the incense and the candles, remove the rest of the items from the table, and put away the stave or wand you used. Alternatively, you can leave the circle active by leaving everything on the table but snuffing out the candles.
21. When you're ready, put everything away.

Bonus: Tree Meditations

Trees have been worshiped throughout history by many cultures, but they've always held a special place of reverence in Celtic traditions. Trees are universally regarded as a symbol of wisdom and life, as they represent a primordial bond that transcends the boundaries of time and civilization. As you've learned in this book, trees have a special significance in Celtic symbolism due to the Celt's close affinity to the natural world. Whether you consider the Celtic Tree calendar being linked with sacred trees or the Ogham script, where each letter has been associated with a particular tree, you'll see trees' importance everywhere in Celtic culture. In fact, the Celts recognized the significance of trees very early on and considered them to be the central axis of their mythology.

Buddha practicing tree meditation.[65]

To them, trees were not merely a source of sustenance, shelter, and warmth but nature's pure essence.

Within the Celtic society, the Druids were believed to have the unique ability to decipher the subtle messages conveyed by Mother Nature. Through these messages, they sought to communicate and interact with the gods and goddesses and even invoke their presence using the ancient sentinels of the forests - the trees. The Celts believed that trees acted as a link between realms in a physical and divine sense. They believed each part of the tree symbolized a different realm, each connected to the other. The trunk of the tree represents the material world, providing people with food, safety, and shelter. The roots went deep into the soil and symbolized the realm of dreams and the latent wisdom of Earth. Finally, the crown and branches of the tree reach skywards, swayed by the wind, which symbolizes the divine plane of consciousness.

The significance of trees in Celtic culture is further proven by the fact that the Druids, who were the highest class among the Celtic people, made their homes among these majestic beings. They rarely ventured into the confines of the villages and instead preferred to stay on the outskirts near the sacred groves where they could be in complete harmony with the trees. Celtic tree meditations are among the most famous rituals of the Celtic culture and hold considerable reverence. Even today, many people choose to practice these guided meditations to connect with their higher consciousness and become harmonious with nature. This bonus chapter will give you a comprehensive list of guided meditations unique to each sacred tree revered in the Celtic world. So, prepare to immerse yourself in the profound wisdom of trees and experience the transformative power of tree meditations.

Birch Tree Meditation

Birch trees are capable of thriving in diverse environments, even in bare soil, and they usually grow in clusters. These ethereal trees are easy to spot due to their white and papery bark. This sturdy tree is not just useful for practical purposes like making furniture but is also very popular from a magical perspective. The outer white bark can be used in rituals to replace paper or parchment, while other parts of the tree are usually used for medicinal purposes. The Birch tree is considered to be one of the three sacred trees for the Druids. In Celtic symbolism, this tree is often called the Goddess Tree, which represents fertility, light, hope, regeneration, and new beginnings. Being a pioneer species, Birch trees have the unique ability to recolonize in case of an ecological disaster, like a forest fire. For this reason, this species is often compared to the Phoenix and linked to rebirth energy in a big way. Birch tree meditation is a wonderful way to enhance your spiritual understanding of Celtic traditions while also gaining insight. If you're starting a new chapter in your life, practicing this meditation is the perfect way to do it.

- Tree meditation is most effective in the presence of the said tree in real time. However, if that's not possible, you can also keep a picture of the tree in front of your meditation space.
- Pick a comfortable position under the tree, or in your meditation space, with your legs crossed. Close your eyes, and take a few deep breaths to ground yourself.
- If you're indoors, a great way to mimic the natural environment is to put on some nature sounds like birds chirping, wind whistling, tree leaves falling, etc.
- Call upon the Birch tree spirit to join you in meditation. Visualize the presence of the Birch spirit standing or sitting beside you, emitting a white light.
- Set your intention by asking these questions, either out loud or silently:
    - Where in my life do I need an infusion of new energy?
    - Where do I need to regenerate?
    - What part of my life has a new chapter coming?
- Once you have finished asking these questions, open your mind and heart to any spiritual guidance you may receive. Be receptive and curious about any intuitions, impressions, or thoughts.
- Take your time in this receptive state and visualize the Birch spirit trying to communicate with you. Take deep, regular breaths, and you might feel a sense of clarity, inspiration, or subtle energy shifts.
- Once you feel you've gotten your guidance, express gratitude to the Birch spirit for joining you in the meditation and guiding you forward.
- Finally, open your eyes, and take a moment to note any impressions, messages, or insights you received during the

meditation session.

- Over the next few days, reflect on the messages you've received while keeping in mind patterns the Birch tree is associated with.
- Also, keep your eyes open for any Birch trees that appear unexpectedly in your surroundings.

Rowan Tree Meditation

The Rowan tree is powerful, with beautiful foliage and ruddy berries. This tree has been associated with protection and magic since ancient times when Druids used to practice tree magic. The tree's bark has significant medicinal benefits and magical uses. Protective charms were frequently carved onto Rowan sticks and placed over windows and doorways to keep evil spirits out. Rune staves, wooden sticks with symbols carved on them, were usually created with Rowan wood. Even the berries that inhabit this tree have protective magic. When the berries are sliced in half, a little pentagram that is related to protective symbols is seen on the interior. The Rowan tree is a tree for all seasons and is especially sacred to most Earth religions. Ancient Celtic legends say Druids would get visions while staying in dedicated Rowan groves. Rowan meditation will help clear your mind, attune to nature, and view the world differently. Rowan is about creativity, intention setting, unconditional love, and astral travel.

- Play calming music that puts you into a dreamy, trance-like state. Get into a comfortable position, and close your eyes.
- Ground and center yourself and breathe into your heart. Inhale, pulling energy up from the earth, and exhale it out in all directions.
- Pull energy up from your crown chakra and breathe it out in all directions. Take a few moments to experience this breath.
- In your mind, travel to a place in nature where you feel peaceful. Visualize that it's winter, and you're dressed warmly.
- From the sky, your spirit horse, all white and mighty, arrives. Take a moment to look at your spirit horse, at the majestic power in its body.
- Imagine yourself mounting your spirit horse and setting off into the sky. Look down at the world from the sky and notice the perspective.

- Take a moment to feel the freedom of flight and let yourself really soar. As you fly high above the earth, your spirit horse will fly to the dimensions of the priestess of Rowan.
- Looking down, you see a landscape filled with beautiful Rowan trees, with their clusters of red and orange berries. You land safely between the trees.
- Dismount your horse and turn your attention to the beautiful grove of Rowan trees. Breathe in the wonderful forest sense, and you'll feel there's inspiration everywhere in this realm full of possibilities.
- Envision a beautiful priestess approaching you from a far-off distance; she comes close to you and places a crown made of Rowan leaves on your head.
- Seek her protective guidance, and she will become your ally. Take time to receive her offerings.
- Show her places in your body, mind, and soul that are distressing you. She will gladly lighten your load and give you inspiration. She will heal you.
- Agree to enlarge your belief system to include more and more of the mystery and magic of creation; connect these to the higher dimensions of love.
- Thank the priestess for her presence in the world. When you're ready, fly back to your world on your spirit horse.
- Take a moment to thank your spirit horse. Ground and center in this space and time. Stay here quietly for a moment and ponder the beauty of your experience!
- Upon returning, write your experiences down in a journal so you don't forget the details of what you felt during your journey.

Alder Tree Meditation

The Alder tree is associated with the spring equinox and symbolizes the evolving spirit. Like birch trees, Alder trees can withstand harsh conditions like swampy locations since their wood doesn't rot when wet. It really hardens when left to sit in water, which the Britons found useful while they were constructing fortresses in early Ireland. The city of Venice itself is said to be built on Alder wood. According to Celtic mythology, Alder trees are associated with the Otherworld, which is where spirits and deities reside. According to another legend, the Alder tree can be used by mediums who want to connect with humans no longer in their physical form. As a result, Druids used to sit in quiet meditation beneath Alder trees and even absorb the flower essence for this purpose.

- Close your eyes and take a few deep breaths to relax and focus. Sit under an Alder tree or in a solitary meditation space.
- Picture roots growing out of your feet and the base of your spine and plant them into the earth. Send them down through all the layers of the earth, branching in all directions.
- Send them down to the earth's center, where a big white ball of energy is located. Now picture this light traveling up through the roots, similar to how roots draw up moisture and sustenance from the earth.
- The energy flows up every root through all the layers of the earth up through the soles of your feet and tailbone. With every breath in, draw this energy up to your heart.
- And as you breathe out, move this energy from your heart down your arms and into your hands; feel the center of your palms get warm.
- With your inhalation, bring the energy back up your arms into your heart and exhale the energy further up through your body and out the crown of your head through your crown chakra.
- As you send this energy out, you observe the energy flowing through the branches going out of your head and shoulders. Send this energy up and up through the sky until it reaches the sun or the moon.
- Feel the energy coursing through your body and feel it energize you.
- Now picture yourself standing in a meadow of lush green grass, the sun is shining bright in the sky, and you feel its warmth and smile.
- You are at peace in the meadow; you see a beautiful creek lined with tall alder trees in the distance. You feel the tall grass swish around your legs.

- You move toward the row of trees and stand under their shade. Looking at the creek, you sense a balance of energy between the water's feminine energy and the trees' masculine energy.
- You feel calm, centered, and completely protected; you turn to face a tree, reach out a hand and place it on the trunk, and feel the bark under your fingers.
- Give your greetings to the tree in whatever way you see fit. Thank the tree for the beautiful energy you feel here today.
- Now sit under the tree; you can even lean against it with your back to it but sit in a comfortable spot and close your eyes.
- Slow your breathing and feel yourself relax; push your awareness outside of yourself and sense the presence of the tree near you.
- Feel how both of your energies become one, a sense that there is no boundary as you merge. What do you feel, see, hear, or maybe smell?
- Once you feel you have made a strong connection with the alder tree, ask the tree a question you need help with or ask for its protective energy for whatever issues you're currently facing.
- Show your gratitude to the alder tree, and once you've received an answer, stand up, and move back into your plane of existence.
- Slowly open your eyes and ground yourself. Write down any insights you gained from the session.

Willow Tree Meditation

The Willow tree usually grows near water, and when nourished properly, it grows quite fast. This tree is representative of spiritual growth and knowledge and offers protection and healing. In folk medicine, the Willow tree has been used to treat various ailments like coughs, fevers, and other inflammatory conditions. Although many people confuse the Willow tree with the Weeping Willow, both trees are different, although resembling each other. Willow tree meditation is used to promote deep healing and help you release your emotional clutter.

- Find a comfortable place where you won't be disturbed for a while. Sit in a comfortable position and take a deep breath. Close your eyes.

- Slowly inhale and exhale. Connect with your environment by feeling the ground beneath you or the scents around you.
- Now visualize a majestic Willow tree in the heat of the summer. The trees are full of green and golden leaves, standing in a stunning field.
- Breathe the air in the field and feel the sun's warmth on your skin. Look at the beautiful droopy leaves of the tree.
- The wind blows them, so they swing gracefully. Watch the birds flying by and caressing the leaves at the branches of the willow.
- Now, think of any issues you're having in your life. Imagine that you pick up the problem and hang it on one of the trees. Let the problem take any physical form you want or no form at all.
- Think of any other problems and repeat the same process. Imagine hanging all your problems on the branches of different willow trees.
- Step about 20 feet back from the Willow trees. Notice how the wind blows the leaves and the problems as they hang on the branches.
- Allow some of the problems to be lifted by the wind and carried away; wave them goodbye as they float away. Take note of the problems that were carried away.
- Now, walk closer to the tree, and imagine that you can actually walk into the trunk of the tree. Feel the effortless weight of the branches and the wind blowing through your leaves.
- Feel that you, as the tree, are strong and that you can let every problem go. Even if some of the issues are still hanging on the branches.
- Feel the calm tranquility of the willow, letting go of your worries with each breeze. When you're ready, you can open your eyes and come back to your space.

Tree meditations have always held a significant place in Celtic spirituality. They provide a unique opportunity to connect with the wisdom and energy of trees, offering a sense of calm and grounding that is unmatched by any other form of meditation. By embracing tree meditations, you can tap into the timeless teachings of nature, fostering tranquility and deepening your understanding of your place in the world.

Conclusion

A single book is not enough to hold the vast knowledge of Celtic mythology, spirituality, and symbolism. Just the symbolism of Celtic culture could be discussed for thousands of pages. In any case, mythology, symbolism, and spirituality are all interconnected, and in order to understand one, it's crucial to understand the other, and so on. From the fascinating history of the Celts to the enigmatic wisdom of the Druids, Celtic lore and symbolism have captured hearts and minds worldwide. Scholars have been studying Celtic symbols in this culture for decades and are still doing so because of the vast meanings and interpretations of the unique and deeply powerful symbols.

What sets Celtic symbolism apart from any other language is that it's not simply ornamental or used for communicative purposes. It holds a deeper significance and wisdom waiting to be discovered. Whether it's the intricate knot work, the majestic animals, or the enigmatic spirals, each symbol has layers and layers of meanings and interpretations that beg for introspection. Take the Celtic Cross as an example, it seems like a simple symbol at first glance, but once you find out its context, the symbol transforms how you look at this world. It represents the interconnectedness of the spiritual and material world and how balance and harmony must be achieved within both. Or consider the Triskele, with its three spirals, symbolizing the eternal cycles of life, death, and rebirth. Each symbol acts as a mirror, reflecting one's life experiences and encouraging one to seek inspiration and a unique worldview.

It is simply not enough to just observe these symbols from a distance. The power of Celtic symbolism lies in its ability to guide and inspire you in parts of your life; simply considering these symbols and their associations as something from history or myth does not help you in any way. Only when you gain actual insight from it that you can apply to your life do you truly fulfill the purpose of these symbols. You must try to infuse your actions, thoughts, and intentions with the essence of these ancient teachings and embrace the deeper meaning behind each symbol. In addition to applying the teachings and interpretations of various symbols into your life, you could also try to integrate the Celtic culture through practical applications like engaging in rituals, practicing spiritual meditation, and immersing yourself in Celtic art and literature. All of these avenues push you toward a stronger connection with the Celts and their rich culture.

As this journey concludes, you should reflect on what you've learned. And continue your quest for knowledge and understanding. There are so many aspects and perspectives about Celtic symbolism and unlimited resources at your fingertips, so why not take this opportunity and learn more about the ancient wisdom of the Celts? May the wisdom of Celtic mythology, spirituality, and symbolism continue to inspire and empower you on your life's journey as you apply these ancient teachings to your own existence; may you find transformation, connection, and a deeper understanding of yourself and the world around you.

If you enjoyed this book, I'd greatly appreciate a review on Amazon because it helps me to create more books that people want. It would mean a lot to hear from you.

To leave a review:

1. Open your camera app.
2. Point your mobile device at the QR code.
3. The review page will appear in your web browser.

Thanks for your support!

Here's another book by Mari Silva that you might like

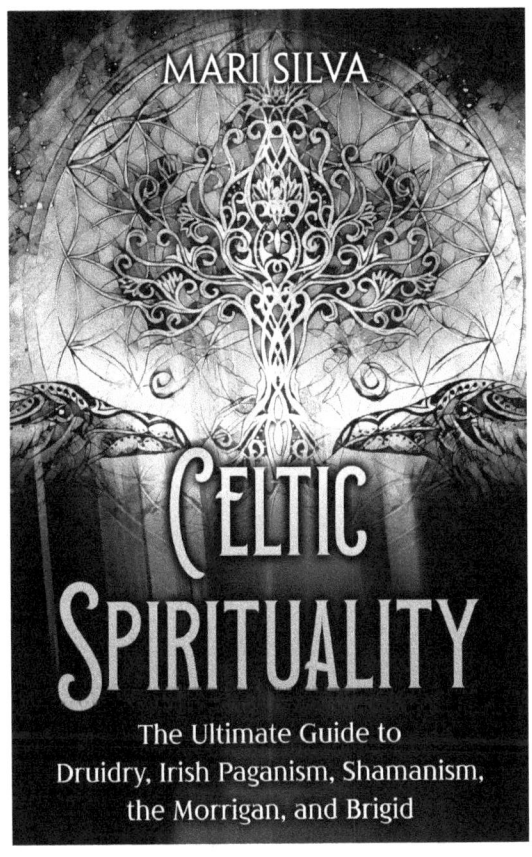

Your Free Gift
(only available for a limited time)

Thanks for getting this book! If you want to learn more about various spirituality topics, then join Mari Silva's community and get a free guided meditation MP3 for awakening your third eye. This guided meditation mp3 is designed to open and strengthen ones third eye so you can experience a higher state of consciousness. Simply visit the link below the image to get started.

https://spiritualityspot.com/meditation

Or, Scan the QR code!

References

Caldwell, R. (2019). Brief history of cartomancy. Academia.edu. https://www.academia.edu/6477311/Brief_history_of_cartomancy

Cicero, C., & Cicero, S. T. (2011). The Essential Golden Dawn: An Introduction to High Magic. Llewellyn Publications.

Decker, R., Depaulis, T., & Dummett, M. (1996). A Wicked Pack of Cards: The Origins of the Occult Tarot. St. Martin's Press.

Decker, R., & Dummett, M. (2013). The History of the Occult Tarot. Prelude Books.

Dunn, P. (2013). Cartomancy with the Lenormand and the Tarot: Create Meaning and Gain Insight from the Cards. Llewellyn Worldwide.

DuQuette, L.M. (2003). Understanding Aleister Crowley's Thoth Tarot. Weiser Books.

Greer, M. K. (2002). Tarot for Your Self: A Workbook for Personal Transformation. New Page Books.

Huson, P. (2004). Mystical Origins of the Tarot: From Ancient Roots to Modern Usage. Destiny Books.

Katz, M., & Goodwin, T. (2011). Around the Tarot in 78 Days: A Personal Journey Through the Cards. Llewellyn Publications.

Keen. (n.d.). Playing card meanings in cartomancy. Keen Articles. Retrieved from https://www.keen.com/articles/tarot/cartomancy-card-meanings

Kliegman, S. (2011). Cartomancy with the Lenormand and the Tarot: Create Meaning & Gain Insight from the Cards. Llewellyn Publications.

Matthews, C. (2014). The Complete Lenormand Oracle Handbook: Reading the Language and Symbols of the Cards. Destiny Books.

McNutt, A., Crisan, A., & Correll, M. (2020, April). Divining insights: Visual analytics through cartomancy. In Extended Abstracts of the 2020 CHI Conference on Human Factors in Computing Systems.

Moore, J. (2012). Cartomancy – Fortune Telling With Playing Cards (Speed Learning Book 1). Kindle Edition.

Moore, B. (2012). Tarot Spreads: Layouts & Techniques to Empower Your Readings. Llewellyn Worldwide.

Nichols, S. (1980). Jung and Tarot: An archetypal journey. Weiser Books.

Pollack, R. (1997). Seventy-Eight Degrees of Wisdom: A Book of Tarot. Thorsons.

Stackpole, M. A. (2006). Cartomancy: Book Two of The Age of Discovery. Spectra.

Waite, A.E. (1910). The Pictorial Key to the Tarot. Rider & Company

(N.d.-e). Ireland-calling.com. https://ireland-calling.com/celtic-mythology-elder-tree/

"The Kelpies": ancient myth in modern art. (n.d.). Artuk.org. https://artuk.org/learn/learning-resources/the-kelpies-ancient-myth-in-modern-art

A Celtic meditation that connects you with the earth--and the ancestors. - Beliefnet. (n.d.). Beliefnet.com. https://www.beliefnet.com/faiths/pagan-and-earth-based/2001/11/the-yew-tree-path-a-meditation.aspx

A Druid Ogham. (n.d.). A Druid Ogham. https://druidogham.wordpress.com/

Ancient Celtic Religion. (n.d.). Tutorialspoint.Com. https://www.tutorialspoint.com/ancient-celtic-religion

Asher, H. (2023, April 8). The moon as a calendar. An Darach Forest Therapy. https://silvotherapy.co.uk/articles/the-moon-as-a-calendar

Beltane. (2015, August 12). By Land, Sea, and Sky. https://thenewpagan.wordpress.com/beltane/

Bhagat, D. (n.d.). The origins and practices of: Samhain, día de los Muertos, and all saints day. Bpl.org. https://www.bpl.org/blogs/post/the-origins-and-practices-of-holidays-samhain-dia-de-los-muertos-and-all-saints-day/

Bot detection! (n.d.). Youglish.com. https://youglish.com/pronounce/yule/english/uk

Brethauer, A. (2021, April 8). Ogham Alphabet Meanings, History, and Divination For Beginners. The Peculiar Brunette. https://www.thepeculiarbrunette.com/ogham-rune-symbol-meanings-history-and-divination-for-beginners/

Brown, C. (2022, November 3). Celtic animism: How mythology can make you a more attentive traveler. Good Nature Travel Blog | Stories Are Made on Adventures; Natural Habitat Adventures.

https://www.nathab.com/blog/celtic-animism-scotland/

Carr-Gomm, S. (2019, December 15). Tree meditation. Order of Bards, Ovates & Druids; OBOD. https://druidry.org/druid-way/teaching-and-practice/meditation/tree-meditation

Carr-Gomm, S. (2019, November 27). Tree lore. Order of Bards, Ovates & Druids; OBOD. https://druidry.org/druid-way/teaching-and-practice/druid-tree-lore

Carstairs, E. (2019, July 11). Ogham divination. Divination Lessons. https://divination-lessons.com/2019/07/11/ogham-divination/

Cartwright, M. (2021). Ancient Celtic religion. World History Encyclopedia. https://www.worldhistory.org/Ancient_Celtic_Religion/

Cartwright, M. (2021). Ancient Celts. World History Encyclopedia. https://www.worldhistory.org/celt/

Celtic deities. (2013, October 14). West Coast Pagan. https://westcoastpagan.com/celtic-reconstructionism/celtic-deities/

Celtic Gods. (n.d.). Mythopedia. https://mythopedia.com/topics/celtic-gods

Celtic mythology — Trees of The CloudForests —. (n.d.). Cloudforests. https://www.cloudforests.ie/trees-of-the-cloudforests/tag/celtic+mythology

Celtic Paganism History, Deities & Facts. (n.d.). Study.Com. https://study.com/academy/lesson/celtic-paganism-history-deities-facts-ancient-religion.html

Celtic Religion – what information do we really have. (n.d.). Murraystate.Edu. http://campus.murraystate.edu/academic/faculty/tsaintpaul/celtreli.html

Celtic tree calendar - my calendar land. (n.d.). Pravljice.org. https://www.pravljice.org/mycalendarland.com/calendar/yearly-calendars/celtic-tree-calendar

Celtic tree month of elder - November 25 - December 22. (n.d.). The Ethical Butcher. https://ethicalbutcher.co.uk/blogs/journal/celtic-tree-month-of-elder-november-25-december-22

Celts. (2017, November 30). HISTORY. https://www.history.com/topics/european-history/celts

Choyt, M. (n.d.). Celtic culture - April: The Alder tree. Celticjewelry.com. https://www.celticjewelry.com/celtic-culture/alder-april

Choyt, M. (n.d.). Celtic culture — Cernunnos, the antlered god of power and blessing. Celticjewelry.com. https://www.celticjewelry.com/celtic-culture/cernunnos

Cross, J. (2019, November 18). Birch Tree meaning and magick. Sanctuary Everlasting. https://www.sanctuaryeverlasting.com/birch-tree-meaning-and-magick/

Dear, R. (1999). Celtic tree calendar: Your tree sign and you. Souvenir Press.

Derrig, J. (2022, July 27). A guide to Celtic Ogham symbols and their meanings. Theirishjewelrycompany.com. https://www.theirishjewelrycompany.com/blog/post/a-guide-to-celtic-ogham-symbols-and-their-meanings

EBK: Bran Fendigaid alias Bendigeitvran, God of Regeneration. (n.d.). Earlybritishkingdoms.com. https://www.earlybritishkingdoms.com/bios/bran.html

Ede-Weaving, M. (2021, May 24). Nature and the Celtic tree calendar. Order of Bards, Ovates & Druids. https://druidry.org/resources/nature-and-the-celtic-tree-calendar

Eilenstein, H. (2018). Cernunnos: Vom Schamanen zum Druiden Merlin. Books on Demand.

Evans, Z. t. (n.d.). Top 5 trees in Celtic mythology, legend and folklore. Folklorethursday.com. https://folklorethursday.com/legends/top-5-trees-in-celtic-mythology-legend-and-folklore/

Every Hawthorn tree has a story. (n.d.). The Present Tree. https://thepresenttree.com/blogs/tree-meanings/every-hawthorn-tree-has-a-story

Fee. (2021, January 18). Older than time: The myth of the Cailleach, the great mother. Wee White Hoose; Fee. https://weewhitehoose.co.uk/study/the-cailleach/

file-uploads/sites/2147611428/video/20407-4274-e6c6-3b2c-f6acf52be077_How_To_Make_An_Ogham_Set_-_Beginners_-_Lora_O_Brien_at_the_Irish_Pagan_School.mp4. (2023, February 2).

Gardiner, B. (2021, November 19). The best guide to understanding the wheel of the year. The Outdoor Apothecary. https://www.outdoorapothecary.com/the-wheel-of-the-year/

Gardiner, B. (2022, May 10). Litha: The incredible history, lore & 20 ways to celebrate. The Outdoor Apothecary. https://www.outdoorapothecary.com/litha/

Hidalgo, S. (2019, June 17). Tree ceremonies and guided meditations for working with the summer season. Llewellyn Worldwide. https://www.llewellyn.com/journal/article/2761

Hislop, I. (2021, April 28). The Celtic Tree of Life meaning & history. ShanOre Irish Jewelry; ShanOre Irish Jewelry. https://www.shanore.com/blog/the-celtic-tree-of-life-meaning-history/

Holly: Legends, customs, and myths. (n.d.). Psu.edu. https://extension.psu.edu/holly-legends-customs-and-myths

How to pronounce ostara? (n.d.). Pronouncenames.com. https://www.pronouncenames.com/Ostara

Irish Around The World. (2019, April 11). The Green Man – an ancient Celtic symbol of rebirth. Irish Around The World. https://irisharoundtheworld.com/the-green-man/

Irish Around The World. (2022, January 19). Top 20 Irish Celtic symbols and their meanings explained. Irish Around The World. https://irisharoundtheworld.com/celtic-symbols/

Irving, J. (2012). Ogham. World History Encyclopedia. https://www.worldhistory.org/Ogham/

Isabella. (n.d.). how to read ogham staves –. WytchenCrafts.

Jay, S. (2022, November 4). 14 Yule traditions & rituals to celebrate winter solstice. Revoloon. https://revoloon.com/shanijay/yule-traditions-rituals-to-celebrate-winter-solstice

Kay, K. (2014, March 17). What's your Celtic tree sign? Find out! Yahoo Life. https://www.yahoo.com/lifestyle/tagged/health/healthy-living/whats-celtic-tree-sign-152200321.html

Kelly, A. (2011, January 7). A month-by-month guide to the Celtic tree calendar – SEE PHOTOS. Irishcentral.com. https://www.irishcentral.com/roots/a-month-by-month-guide-to-the-celtic-tree-calendar-see-photos-113064709-237735251

Khaliela. (2022, February 2). Rowan meditation. Khaliela Wright. https://khalielawright.com/rowan-meditation/

King, J. (2019). Celtic warfare. World History Encyclopedia. https://www.worldhistory.org/Celtic_Warfare/

Lang, D. (2018, August 18). Ogham as a Practice. Esoteric Moment. https://esotericmoment.com/2018/08/18/ogham-as-a-practice/

LetsGoIreland. (2022, January 5). Celtic Symbols: Your complete guide to the Origins and meanings. Let's Go Ireland. https://www.letsgoireland.com/celtic-symbols-and-meanings/

LetsGoIreland. (2022, March 15). Celtic Tree of Life: Complete Guide to the Origin and Meaning. Let's Go Ireland. https://www.letsgoireland.com/celtic-tree-of-life/

LetsGoIreland. (2023, May 18). Celtic Tree of Life tattoo meaning and significance. Let's Go Ireland. https://www.letsgoireland.com/celtic-tree-of-life-tattoo-meaning/

LibGuides: Brigid: About. (2021). https://westportlibrary.libguides.com/brigid

LibGuides: Brigid: About. (2021). https://westportlibrary.libguides.com/brigid

Loh-Hagan, V. (2020). Celtic tree astrology. 45th Parallel Press.

Lor, H. O. (2021, September 24). The Tree of Life Symbol meaning. House Of Lor | Irish Jewellery | Pure Gold from Ireland; House of Lor Jewellery. https://houseoflor.com/the-tree-of-life-symbol/

Mark, J. J. (2019). Wheel of the Year. World History Encyclopedia. https://www.worldhistory.org/Wheel_of_the_Year/

Meditation with Trees. (n.d.). Viajealasostenibilidad.org. https://viajealasostenibilidad.org/meditation-with-trees/

Miller, F. P., Vandome, A. F., & McBrewster, J. (Eds.). (2010). Imbolc. Alphascript Publishing.

Month 3: Alder Tree Meditation. (n.d.). SoundCloud. https://soundcloud.com/nicola-mcintosh-52427282/alder-meditation

Mulhern, K. (n.d.). What is the Wheel of the Year? Patheos.com. https://www.patheos.com/answers/what-is-the-wheel-of-the-year

Neal, C. F. (2015). Imbolc: Rituals, recipes and lore for Brigid's day. Llewellyn Publications.

No title. (n.d.). Com.Eg. https://www.twinkl.com.eg/teaching-wiki/celtic-knot-meanings

No title. (n.d.). Study.com. https://study.com/learn/lesson/animism-beliefs-practices-thinking.html

No title. (n.d.). Twinkl.com. https://www.twinkl.com/teaching-wiki/the-celts

No title. (n.d.-a). Study.com. https://study.com/learn/lesson/yggrasil-tree-of-life.html

No title. (n.d.-b). Com.Eg. https://www.twinkl.com.eg/teaching-wiki/celtic-knot-meanings

O'Hara, K. (2023, January 2). The Morrigan: The story of the fiercest goddess in Irish myth. The Irish Road Trip. https://www.theirishroadtrip.com/the-morrigan/

O'Hara, K. (2023, June 1). Celtic Tree of Life (Crann Bethadh) meaning. The Irish Road Trip. https://www.theirishroadtrip.com/celtic-tree-of-life-symbol/

O'Hara, K. (2023a, May 29). 15 Celtic symbols and meanings (an Irishman's 2023 guide). The Irish Road Trip. https://www.theirishroadtrip.com/celtic-symbols-and-meanings/

O'Hara, K. (2023b, June 3). Trinity knot / Triquetra symbol: Meaning + history. The Irish Road Trip. https://www.theirishroadtrip.com/the-triquetra-celtic-trinity-knot/

Ogham alphabet. (n.d.). Omniglot.com. https://omniglot.com/writing/ogham.htm

Ogham Discipline: Understanding Your Connection. (n.d.). Ogham.Academy. https://www.ogham.academy/blog/ogham-discipline

Ogham Divination in The Summerlands. (n.d.). Summerlands.Com. http://www.summerlands.com/crossroads/library/oghamdiv.htm

Ogham Meditation Ritual. (2014, September 30). Ogham Divination. https://oghamdivination.wordpress.com/what-is-ogham/ogham-meditation-ritual/

Ogham: Ireland's original alphabet. (n.d.). Shamrock Gift. https://www.shamrockgift.com/blog/ogham/

Olsen, E. (2022, June 21). 13 Celtic Tree Months –. Celebrate Pagan Holidays. https://www.celebratepaganholidays.com/general/13-celtic-tree-months

Ostara (Spring Equinox) - the wiccan calendar -. (2017, June 13). Wicca Living. https://wiccaliving.com/wiccan-calendar-ostara-spring-equinox/

Ostara / spring equinox. (2015, August 16). By Land, Sea and Sky. https://thenewpagan.wordpress.com/ostara-spring-equinox/

Pagan, W. C. (2019a, June 14). Litha / Midsummer. West Coast Pagan. https://westcoastpagan.com/2019/06/13/litha-midsummer/

Pagan, W. C. (2019b, August 14). Lughnasadh / lammas. West Coast Pagan. https://westcoastpagan.com/2019/08/13/lughnasadh-lammas/

Pagan, W. C. (2019c, September 14). Mabon / autumn equinox. West Coast Pagan. https://westcoastpagan.com/2019/09/13/mabon-autumn-equinox/

Park, G. K. (2020). animism. In Encyclopedia Britannica.

Rajchel, D. (2015). Samhain: Rituals, Recipes & Lore for Halloween. Llewellyn Publications. https://thenewpagan.wordpress.com/wheel-of-the-year/samhain/

Rhys, D. (2021, August 13). Celtic sailor's knot - what does it symbolize? Symbol Sage. https://symbolsage.com/celtic-sailors-knot/

Rhys, D. (2021, July 29). Ogham symbols and their meaning - A list. Symbol Sage. https://symbolsage.com/ogham-symbols-and-their-meaning/

Rogador, C. (2020, June 28). The Celtic Triskele: History and meaning. Ireland Travel Guides. https://irelandtravelguides.com/celtic-triskele-history-meaning/

Rogador, C. (2021, June 9). The Celtic knots (different types and meanings). Ireland Travel Guides. https://irelandtravelguides.com/celtic-knot-history/

Sempers, C. (2002a). The Celtic tree calendar. Corvus Books.

Sempers, C. (2002b). The Celtic tree calendar. Corvus Books.

Silva, T. (2022, October 12). Alder tree symbolism and meanings. Grooving Trees. https://www.groovingtrees.com/alder-tree-symbolism

Sinclair, A. (2021, December 10). Celtic Tree Astrology: Zodiac signs & birthday horoscopes. Oak Hill Gardens. https://www.oakhillgardens.com/blog/celtic-tree-astrology-zodiac-signs-birthday-horoscopes

Soul, M. M. (2019). Imbolc: Witch's Journal & Workbook. Independently Published.

Stanton, K. M. (2022, December 1). Tree of Life meaning, symbolism, and mythology. UniGuide®; Kristen M. Stanton. https://www.uniguide.com/tree-of-life

Storey, L. (2018, October 19). Know a thing or two... Trees and druid traditions. The Simple Things. https://www.thesimplethings.com/blog/know-a-thing-or-two-trees-druid-traditions

Tailtiu: Harvest goddess. (n.d.). Goddess-pages.co.uk. https://goddess-pages.co.uk/galive/issue-18-home/tailtiu-harvest-goddess/

The Cauldron in Celtic life. (n.d.). Irelandseye.com. http://www.irelandseye.com/aarticles/culture/talk/superstitions/cauldron.shtm

The Celtic wheel of the year —. (n.d.). The Path of Integrity. https://thepathofintegrity.com/celtic-wheel

The Editors of Encyclopedia Britannica. (2018). Belenus. In Encyclopedia Britannica.

The Ogham alphabet. (n.d.). Ogham.Ie. https://ogham.ie/history/ogham-alphabet/

The Sacred Fire – Ancient Celtic Cosmology. (n.d.). Sacredfire.Net. https://www.sacredfire.net/cosmology.html

The Sacredness of Nature. (2012, March 22). The Druid Network.

The Song of Amergin: Modern English translation. (n.d.). Thehypertexts.com. http://www.thehypertexts.com/Song%20of%20Amergin%20Modern%20English%20Translation.htm

The tree meditation. (2013, May 2). The Druid Network.

The Tree of Life – an ancient Celtic symbol. (2021, September 26). Irish Urns. https://irishurns.com/the-tree-of-life-an-ancient-celtic-symbol/

Top 30+ Celtic symbols and their meanings (updated monthly). (n.d.). 1000logos.net. https://1000logos.net/top-30-celtic-symbols-and-their-meaning/

Traditions, I. (2016, July 24). Irish Traditions: The Celtic Tree of Life. Irish Traditions - A Tipperary Store; Irish Traditions. https://irishtraditionsonline.com/celtic-tree-of-life/

Tree of Life symbol: This image appears in many Irish expressions! (n.d.). Irish Expressions. https://www.irish-expressions.com/tree-of-life-symbol.html

We'Moon. (n.d.). Beltane rituals and traditions. We'Moon. https://wemoon.ws/blogs/pagan-holiday-traditions/beltane

What's your tree sign according to Celtic tree astrology. (2015, September 23). Fantastic Gardeners Blog. https://blog.fantasticgardeners.co.uk/whats-your-tree-sign-according-to-celtic-tree-astrology/

Wheel of the Year. (2013, June 22). The Celtic Journey. https://thecelticjourney.wordpress.com/the-celts/wheel-of-the-year/

Who were the Celts? (n.d.). Twinkl. https://www.twinkl.com/teaching-wiki/the-celts

Who were the Druids? (2017, March 21). Historic UK. https://www.historic-uk.com/HistoryUK/HistoryofWales/Druids/

Wigington, P. (2008, June 2). The Celtic Ogham Symbols. Learn Religions. https://www.learnreligions.com/ogham-symbol-gallery-4123029

Wigington, P. (2008, June 2). The Celtic Ogham Symbols. Learn Religions. https://www.learnreligions.com/ogham-symbol-gallery-4123029

Wigington, P. (2011, September 18). Get to know the magic of the Celtic tree calendar. Learn Religions. https://www.learnreligions.com/celtic-tree-months-2562403

Wigington, P. (2014a, March 19). Beltane Rites and Rituals. Learn Religions. https://www.learnreligions.com/beltane-rites-and-rituals-2561678

Wigington, P. (2014b, June 21). Rites, rituals, and ways to celebrate Mabon, the autumn equinox. Learn Religions. https://www.learnreligions.com/mabon-rites-and-rituals-2562284

Will the real Lúnasa / Lughnasa / lughnasadh please stand up? (2010, August 1). Irish Language Blog | Language and Culture of the Irish-Speaking World; Irish Language Blog. https://blogs.transparent.com/irish/will-the-real-lunasa-lughnasa-lughnasadh-please-stand-up/

Williams, S. (2014, May 10). Celtic zodiac: Vine tree. Sun Signs. https://www.sunsigns.org/celtic-astrology-vine-tree/

Yule / Midwinter. (2015, August 27). By Land, Sea and Sky. https://thenewpagan.wordpress.com/wheel-of-the-year/yule-midwinter

Image Sources

[1] https://unsplash.com/photos/7s2ip7OVktg

[2] *Asimzb Edit By Jfitch, CC BY 3.0 <https://creativecommons.org/licenses/by/3.0>, via Wikimedia Commons: https://commons.wikimedia.org/wiki/File:Playing_cards-Edit1.jpg*

[3] https://unsplash.com/fr/photos/carte-a-jouer-dame-de-pique-OfdFHy1zxjQ?utm_content=creditCopyText&utm_medium=referral&utm_source=unsplash

[4] https://commons.wikimedia.org/wiki/File:1890_German_Lenormand_card.jpg

[5] *Tcg8888, CC BY-SA 4.0 <https://creativecommons.org/licenses/by-sa/4.0>, via Wikimedia Commons: https://commons.wikimedia.org/wiki/File:Kipper_Cards.jpg*

[6] https://unsplash.com/photos/_MuYSOlPcWc

[7] https://unsplash.com/photos/QdmMWxQXJ2Y

[8] *WolfgangRieger, CC0, via Wikimedia Commons: https://commons.wikimedia.org/wiki/File:3-Card-Spread.svg*

[9] *WolfgangRieger, CC0, via Wikimedia Commons: https://commons.wikimedia.org/wiki/File:Celtic_Cross_Spread_-_Waite.svg*

[10] https://unsplash.com/photos/dttmeqFUDSU

[11] https://unsplash.com/photos/GK8FMN7xJXQ?utm_source=unsplash&utm_medium=referral&utm_content=creditShareLink

[12] https://commons.wikimedia.org/wiki/File:Print,_playing-card_(BM_1982,U.4598.1-78_09).jpg

[13] https://unsplash.com/photos/j5itydU55FI

[14] https://commons.wikimedia.org/wiki/File:RWS_Tarot_10_Wheel_of_Fortune.jpg

[15] *Museum Rotterdam, CC BY-SA 3.0 <https://creativecommons.org/licenses/by-sa/3.0>, via Wikimedia Commons: https://commons.wikimedia.org/wiki/File:Spel_handgeschreven_kaarten_met_spreuken,_objectnr_32256.JPG*

[16] *OxYm3rioN, CC BY-SA 4.0 <https://creativecommons.org/licenses/by-sa/4.0>, via Wikimedia Commons: https://commons.wikimedia.org/wiki/File:Celts_in_Europe-fr.png*

[17] https://unsplash.com/photos/axYekjy6Kn4

¹⁸ https://commons.wikimedia.org/wiki/File:Awen_symbol_final.svg

¹⁹ Imbolc.cerddwr, CC BY-SA 3.0 <https://creativecommons.org/licenses/by-sa/3.0>, via Wikimedia Commons: https://commons.wikimedia.org/wiki/File:Wheel_of_the_year.png

²⁰ Culnacreann, CC BY 3.0 <https://creativecommons.org/licenses/by/3.0>, via Wikimedia Commons: https://commons.wikimedia.org/wiki/File:Saint_Brigid%27s_cross.jpg

²¹ Jpbowen at the English-language Wikipedia, CC BY-SA 3.0 <http://creativecommons.org/licenses/by-sa/3.0/>, via Wikimedia Commons: https://commons.wikimedia.org/wiki/File:Bowen_knot.jpg

²² https://commons.wikimedia.org/wiki/File:Triskele-Symbol-spiral-five-thirds-turns.svg

²³ Otourly, CC BY-SA 3.0 <https://creativecommons.org/licenses/by-sa/3.0>, via Wikimedia Commons: https://commons.wikimedia.org/wiki/File:Horned-God-Symbol.svg

²⁴ https://commons.wikimedia.org/wiki/File:Trefoil-triquetra-circular-arcs-around-triangle_(solid).svg

²⁵ Madboy74, CC BY-SA 4.0 <https://creativecommons.org/licenses/by-sa/4.0>, via Wikimedia Commons: https://commons.wikimedia.org/wiki/File:Coa_Illustration_Cross_Carolingian.svg

²⁶ Shii (Communications Officer, Reformed Druids of Carleton College), CC0, via Wikimedia Commons: https://commons.wikimedia.org/wiki/File:Reformed_Druids.svg

²⁷ AnonMoos (initial SVG conversion of PostScript source by AnonMoos was done by Indolences), Public domain, via Wikimedia Commons: https://commons.wikimedia.org/wiki/File:Triquetra-circle-interlaced.svg

²⁸ https://unsplash.com/photos/vUNQaTiZeOo?utm_source=unsplash&utm_medium=referral&utm_content=creditShareLink

²⁹ https://unsplash.com/photos/oSaq0J4zGE0?utm_source=unsplash&utm_medium=referral&utm_content=creditShareLink

³⁰ https://unsplash.com/photos/oSaq0J4zGE0?utm_source=unsplash&utm_medium=referral&utm_content=creditShareLink

³¹ https://www.pexels.com/photo/smoke-coming-from-iron-cauldron-16010709/

³² https://commons.wikimedia.org/wiki/File:Celtic_cross.svg

³³ Miguel Mendez from Malahide, Ireland, CC BY 2.0 <https://creativecommons.org/licenses/by/2.0>, via Wikimedia Commons: https://commons.wikimedia.org/wiki/File:Claddagh_ring_(7061237901).jpg

³⁴ https://unsplash.com/photos/FGkNt8tO04I?utm_source=unsplash&utm_medium=referral&utm_content=creditShareLink

³⁵ Rosser1954, CC BY-SA 4.0 <https://creativecommons.org/licenses/by-sa/4.0>, via Wikimedia Commons: https://commons.wikimedia.org/wiki/File:Green_Man_water_feature.jpg

³⁶ https://unsplash.com/photos/NumcxeDrWUQ?utm_source=unsplash&utm_medium=referral&utm_content=creditShareLink

³⁷ original raster image and vector PostScript source code by AnonMoos, initial vectorization by Erin Silversmith, Public domain, via Wikimedia Commons: https://commons.wikimedia.org/wiki/File:Triquetra-Double.svg

[38] *Madboy74, CC BY-SA 4.0 <https://creativecommons.org/licenses/by-sa/4.0>, via Wikimedia Commons:* https://commons.wikimedia.org/wiki/File:Coa_Illustration_Taranis_Wheel.svg

[39] *Symbols illustrated by Jasmina El Bouamraoui and Karabo Poppy Moletsane, CC0, via Wikimedia Commons:* https://commons.wikimedia.org/wiki/File:Wikipedia20_background_Lunar_cycle.jpg

[40] https://commons.wikimedia.org/wiki/File:Ogham_Key_Anderson_1881b_Fig_133_scotlandinearlyc00anderich_0254.jpg

[41] https://commons.wikimedia.org/wiki/File:Ogham_letter_beith.svg

[42] https://commons.wikimedia.org/wiki/File:Ogham_letter_luis.svg

[43] https://commons.wikimedia.org/wiki/File:Ogham_letter_fearn.svg

[44] https://commons.wikimedia.org/wiki/File:Ogham_letter_sail.svg

[45] https://commons.wikimedia.org/wiki/File:Ogham_letter_nion.svg

[46] https://commons.wikimedia.org/wiki/File:Ogham_letter_uath.svg

[47] https://commons.wikimedia.org/wiki/File:Ogham_letter_dair.svg

[48] https://commons.wikimedia.org/wiki/File:Ogham_letter_tinne.svg

[49] https://commons.wikimedia.org/wiki/File:Ogham_letter_coll.svg

[50] https://commons.wikimedia.org/wiki/File:Ogham_letter_ceirt.svg

[51] https://commons.wikimedia.org/wiki/File:Ogham_letter_muin.svg

[52] https://commons.wikimedia.org/wiki/File:Ogham_letter_gort.svg

[53] https://commons.wikimedia.org/wiki/File:Ogham_letter_ngeadal.svg

[54] https://commons.wikimedia.org/wiki/File:Ogham_letter_straif.svg

[55] https://commons.wikimedia.org/wiki/File:Ogham_letter_ruis.svg

[56] https://commons.wikimedia.org/wiki/File:Ogham_letter_ailm.svg

[57] https://commons.wikimedia.org/wiki/File:Ogham_letter_onn.svg

[58] https://commons.wikimedia.org/wiki/File:Ogham_letter_ur.svg

[59] https://commons.wikimedia.org/wiki/File:Ogham_letter_eadhadh.svg

[60] https://commons.wikimedia.org/wiki/File:Ogham_letter_iodhadh.svg

[61] https://commons.wikimedia.org/wiki/File:Wheel_of_the_Year.svg

[62] *Art Gongs, CC BY-SA 4.0 <https://creativecommons.org/licenses/by-sa/4.0>, via Wikimedia Commons:* https://commons.wikimedia.org/wiki/File:Celtic_Tree_Of_Life_Art_Gong.jpg

[63] https://www.pexels.com/photo/anonymous-person-standing-on-footpath-in-autumn-6272345/

[64] https://www.pexels.com/photo/anonymous-female-soothsayers-with-crystal-ball-and-tarot-card-during-divination-session-6944350/

[65] *Thomas Nordwest, CC BY-SA 4.0 <https://creativecommons.org/licenses/by-sa/4.0>, via Wikimedia Commons:* https://commons.wikimedia.org/wiki/File:Buddha_in_Meditation_2023-05-11-22.jpg

www.ingramcontent.com/pod-product-compliance
Lightning Source LLC
Chambersburg PA
CBHW051854160426
43209CB00006B/1289